What on Earth is the Church?

What on EARTH is the CHURCH?

An Inquirer's Guide

Robert Thornton Henderson

Foreword by William Pannell

WIPF & STOCK · Eugene, Oregon

WHAT ON EARTH IS THE CHURCH?
An Inquirer's Guide

Copyright © 2016 Robert Thornton Henderson. All rights reserved. Except for brief quotations in critical publications or reviews, no part of this book may be reproduced in any manner without prior written permission from the publisher. Write: Permissions, Wipf and Stock Publishers, 199 W. 8th Ave., Suite 3, Eugene, OR 97401.

Wipf & Stock
An Imprint of Wipf and Stock Publishers
199 W. 8th Ave., Suite 3
Eugene, OR 97401

www.wipfandstock.com

PAPERBACK ISBN 13: 978-1-4982-3885-4
HARDCOVER ISBN 13: 978-1-4982-3887-8

Manufactured in the U.S.A.   04/22/2016

CONTENTS

Foreword by William Pannell | vii
Preface | xi

1 What on Earth Is the Church? | 1
2 Where You Would Probably Not Look | 6
3 Jesus the Rock: His Messianic Message and Mission | 21
4 What on Earth Are You Looking For? (And What Are You Not?) | 28
5 The Door and the Disciplines | 40
6 The Church: Its Form and Function | 51
7 Models and Mentors | 62
8 The Mystery Behind the Mystery | 75
9 The Worldliness of Worship | 93
   Epilogue: The Church: The Aroma of Christ | 103

FOREWORD

Bob Henderson is a friend. He is also uniquely qualified to write on this subject, what with his long career of engaging racial, cultural, and generational challenges redemptively. He is also a colleague in ministry. We go back many years since I first preached in his Presbyterian congregation in New Orleans. I found him to be a raconteur of Basin Street, and I learned to respect his love of the city and comfort among African Americans in that city. I have enjoyed his company and his good humor. I was not surprised when his (privately published) memoir was entitled *Journey into Laughter*. So we have followed each other around the country, kept in touch through mutual friends in that important network from the 60s, where being *evangelical*, no matter what one's affiliation was, took a toll. After all, we were churchmen and as such were often seen to be on the wrong side of town during those turbulent days of civil rights activism. Small wonder that someone from those days would write about the church and wonder, "why in the world is the church?" The writer was not from the side of town where Black believers lived and worshiped, demonstrating their understanding of that question. (It was that splendid editor of *The Carolina Israelite* who argued that the Black church had saved Christianity in America.)

The question would not go away even though those who ostensibly professed to know the answer, namely the councils of church and the so-called mainline denominations in America, had seemingly confused the sequence affecting the issue. Those professed leaders of the churches dominated the debate and struggled to coordinate the *why* and the *what* of the church's identity and its mission in the world. Lesslie Newbigin had waged his polemic war in international ecclesial circles, producing a fine lecture series entitled *The Household of God* in the late 1950s. He focused on the nature of the church. The *what* of the church proceeds in importance the *why* of the church, he argued.

But that was then; this is now. So why would Bob Henderson write about the same stuff? Why go over the ground that so many others, then and now, have plowed? Or is this that? Well, yes and no. Readers of a certain age will recognize his handling of the topic as he carefully works his way through Scripture references. He does this because he knows the church today is biblically illiterate when it comes to an understanding of its identity from the divine point of view.

Currently, one would get the impression that *church* is defined by the notoriety of its leaders—often its more flamboyant pastors and hucksters of gospels suited to television's influence. Another way of saying this might be to observe that that those who will recognize the *why* of his writing are aging, and they are painfully aware that their understanding of church is not the same as the younger generation, who, in their view, are stealing the church from them. This is a generational issue of course, and this really sets the stage for this writing.

This is new turf and a new army of young people occupies it. They face questions that an older generation could hardly imagine. They are joined with their counterparts worldwide who surf and tweet each other with self-images depicting joy and grief, hope and despair never seen on such a global scale. These young people have one thing in common, though they do not always recognize it: *religion* is at the core of their shared existence. Religion dominates the political agenda affecting their futures. This is especially true in most of the European continent, and from Africa to Afghanistan.

The young people most likely to be ignorant of this are Americans. But even here the culture is haunted by religion. Oprah could

Foreword

comment that "I knew . . . Jesus would show up sooner or later" at one of her fabulous parties, "and He did in song and dance. But he wasn't invited." The same could be said of the churches, even those that still dominate communities where African Americans dominate. The buildings are still there and Sunday is still an important day in the life of thousands. Meanwhile, there are millions—a whole generation, especially these young adults—for whom the church is just a building full of aging folks from . . . somewhere. The members often live elsewhere, beyond old boundaries that defined community and ethnic identity. We are becoming a nation of religious orphans.

So Henderson, holding his coffee cup in one hand, and with a smile on his face, engages this generation about a topic always on his heart, and often on theirs. His tone is warm, friendly, engaging. He is smart but hides it well; too much is at stake here to be glib. This is a book about friends who are deeply concerned to understand the meaning of the church in our time. It is an engaging conversation and worthy of wide acceptance. What does it mean to be the people of God at the end of this age?

William Pannell
Professor of Preaching Emeritus
Founding Director of the African-American Studies Program
Fuller Theological Seminary

PREFACE

Let me tell you what has motivated me to write this book (and if you're not interested, then just skip it and go on to chapter 1).

What is behind this book is that I am, maybe, a slow learner, and it has slowly dawned on me how much confusion there is about that entity known as *the church*. I say "slowly" because I was beginning to see this sixty years ago when I was involved in the church's ministry to university and college students, and they were at that age when they were not afraid to question the dimensions of the Christian faith with which they had grown up—nor were they the least bit intimidated by me with all of my "clergy credentials."

Later, when I was pastoring a very lively church next to a university campus, and we were seeking to equip our members to engage their daily experiences with the mission of God, many of our student participants, upon graduation, found that our small church on the edge of the North Carolina city of Durham was something of a rarity, and they were dismayed that so many of the churches they had investigated in their new locations were only focused on the church's own inner life and activities, and were too often quite irrelevant to the daily discipleship in which they were engaged.

I began to get more and more communications from those alumni, out of our particular church community, asking my help in understanding what it was that created such a nurturing and equipping community such as ours was to them. To that end, as

Preface

long ago as 1986, I wrote a book for them to which my publisher gave the title *Beating the Churchgoing Blahs*.[1] This made the rounds, and is now long since out of print. In the intervening years, however, I have grown into something of a resident *contrarian*, or maybe an annoying *gadfly*, as my career as pastor and teacher has led me into a diversity of church situations, and where I have sought (I modestly admit) to bring some light to this familiar ecclesiastical darkness with several more books.

What has been somewhat dismaying is that I have discovered how that even those who are emotionally wedded to their own particular church community engagement seem so often to have no clear sense of the reason for the church's calling, i.e., no concept the church's beautiful purpose in the mission of Jesus, or of the disciplines that Christ has mandated, which are so essential if such colonies of God's *new humanity* is to fulfill the purpose of that calling. This ecclesiastical confusion has produced many passive observers, or folk who simply like the *churchy ethos* as it is, and who may be enthusiastic supporters of their local church institution . . . but are somewhat mindless and unaware of how the church is to be (to borrow from our Latin American friends) "the missionary arm of the Holy Trinity." They are a long way from any existential engagement with anything like Dietrich Bonhoeffer's memorable word, "When Jesus calls a man, he bids him come and die."[2]

So now, here in my octogenarian years, I find myself in regular conversation with those of the emerging generations (Gen Y and Gen Z) who are many decades younger than I and who energize me with their own questions and quests. They are the products of a totally different, post-Christian, social-media saturated, in-transition culture . . . in which the church, and its in-house jargon (so familiar to my own generation), are an unknown—it simply doesn't register. When I sit in the coffee shops or pubs and engage such wonderful young men and women of this emerging

---

1. Robert Thornton Henderson, *Beating the Churchgoing Blahs* (Downers Grove, IL: InterVarsity, 1986).

2. Dietrich Bonhoeffer, *The Cost of Discipleship*, translated by R. H. Fuller (New York: Macmillan, 1949), 87.

Preface

and unique generation, I realize that my world is a whole different one than that with which they are familiar. And yet, at the same time, they are subconsciously questing for the very meaning and hope and acceptance that Jesus came to make real in the world of lost and confused men and women, whom he loved.

It is such persons who are the primary audience of this book.

I'm intrigued by an emerging generation that has access to more information than any generation ever.[3] This is an emerging generation who are entrepreneurial, change-focused, digitally overconnected, and yet not precise communicators. It is these who may even have a difficult time comprehending the phenomenon known as *the church*—the theme that surfaces so regularly in our conversations, especially when they ask me what my career has been. When I say something like the fact that I have been a *pastor* to the *church*, they may not have a clue what I'm talking about, but they're really kind to this old guy. Yet it is not at all unusual for them to ask me, first, "What in the world is a *pastor*?," then secondly, "What in the world is the *church* all about?" I am aware that for me to even attempt to write to such is, for me, an exercise in cross-cultural communication at which I can only give my best shot.

Then, to many of those who have had some contact with the church, it has often been, maybe, confusing or something of an off-putting experience, and they can be a bit cautious if not downright cynical about it. Yes, to others there are very positive associations. But it is still to some a total enigma, to some a stumbling block, to some an embarrassment . . . and yet to others something that speaks to their quest for relationships and community. Then to some of my conversation partners it is a topic they don't even want to approach, so they change the subject to Saturday's football game. Some are embittered by a previous encounter—but they will

---

3. The generation born after 1995, and designated as Generation Z, or the iY Generation, and numbering some twenty-three million, has been also described as entrepreneurial, change focused, digitally overconnected, and as not precise communicators. Those generalizations are just that: generalizations. Individuals are still individuals with their own personalities, experiences, and cultural frameworks.

raise the subject of their encounters with the church . . . and they come at me from so many different directions: non-comprehension, longing, hostility, consternation, inquisitiveness, or maybe blinded by its contradictions.

This is a generation that is emerging fully into the *post-Christian era*, and the church has not usually been a formative part of their lives, though they may have found new life and hope in Jesus and his teachings. It is several of these younger persons who have encouraged me to write something that will give them some clues. What a challenge!

Here is this entity called *the church*, which Jesus said that he himself was going to build . . . and here we are after two full millennia into what is known as the *Christian Era* (e.g., 2015 CE). What has transpired in all of those multiple generations has produced so many positive and negative episodes. What is so often looked at by the media, unfortunately, are the contradictory behaviors of those professing to be the church, which can be destructive, bitter, divisive, incomprehensible, and indefensible, what with folks getting hostile to those who disagree with them, or maybe getting burned at the stake over a difference of interpretation—that sort of thing.

But then, how to explain in the face of all the negatives, that even as there have been those embarrassing and contradictory episodes, there has been that huge host of Christ's disciples quietly demonstrating grace and love and justice and hope and hospitality and generosity and humanitarian ministries almost unnoticed, and a church that has continued to grow and transform lives and communities around the globe even in the face of unbelievable opposition?

One needs a great deal of humor to engage the subject of the church. I mean, look at the unlikely folk that Jesus calls to be part of this church—folk in all degrees of maturity and immaturity, folk fractured and captive to all kinds of devious inner demons. None perfect, none worthy on their own merits, none who can boast of their own arrival apart from the grace of God in Jesus Christ. So what are we to make of the church phenomenon that we have inherited here in the twenty-first century?

Preface

On the one hand, what I am engaging here may be an exercise in *semiotics*, i.e., what does the church signify to those who, however superficially, may engage its reality. On the other hand, the request that my young colleagues have made of me reminds me of the task assigned to the art restorers several years back: restoring Michelangelo's masterpiece, *The Creation*, painted on the ceiling of the Sistine Chapel at the Vatican. What the restorers discovered was that centuries of candle smoke and the resultant layer of soot, plus the well-meaning but misdirected zeal of some later artists who thought Michelangelo a bit too immodest in his portrayals of nude figures, and so painted over some delicate parts of the masterpiece, had obscured the brilliance of the original. I cannot imagine the challenges they must have faced, having visited the Sistine Chapel and having seen how vast is that painting. Yet with incredible patience and skill they removed the layers of soot and the later paint-overs and restored it to its pristine condition. It emerged once again brilliant and overwhelming in its original.

Or maybe what I am being asked to do is like what one encounters when an architectural masterpiece, after generations of additions, decay, or alterations that have violated its basic integrity—or maybe also overgrown with vines—is then rediscovered and skillfully restored to its original integrity, to the wonder of all. I know that I am being unforgivably presumptuous in assuming such a project, and I also know that many others have engaged it most helpfully, and to many of them I am indebted. At the same time, I am compelled to pursue this in a quest to set forth the church as a brilliant and critical dimension of the gospel of the kingdom of God, of God's New Creation. I often describe my role as that of both *archaeologist* and *architect*. My design is to retrieve the treasures of the church's legacy over the centuries, but also to seek an alternative narrative for its encounter with the realities of the twenty-first century. Both are necessary.

For all of the contradictory and confusing encumbrances that can obscure Jesus' purpose for his church, I am altogether persuaded that the church is a thrilling part of the joyous news of Jesus Christ, that it is to be that *community of the age to come*. It

Preface

is God's design that *"through us [God] spreads the fragrance of the knowledge of him everywhere. For we are the aroma of him [Christ] . . ."* (2 Cor 2:14–15 ESV). I am fascinated by the reality that the church, made up of such folk as you and I, is actually to be the beautiful Bride of Christ, and so to be fully identified with him at the consummation of all things. I am convinced that the church is intended to be the missionary arm of the Holy Trinity. And I can never quite grasp the awesome description by the apostle that the church is "the *dwelling place of God by the Holy Spirit*" (Ephesians 2:22 paraphrase).

This all being so, come and walk with me through some of the landscape, which we inherit, and look at some very obvious designs that emerge from Scripture (that are too often go unnoticed). If I have learned a few things that will be helpful to the next generation and have some modicum of wisdom to share, I am thrilled. Add to that my continual amazement at how relentlessly so many of my young friends are able to see through all of the "ecclesiastical crap" that escapes the notice of so many older observers. We will make some discoveries that everything that pertains to be the church . . . may *not* be so at all, and conversely, some things that get below radar may be the Spirit's most dramatic working in the creation of the church. Yes, let's take a walk. Join me.

Of necessity and in an attempt at some brevity, I will often paint in broad strokes, since the task is so large (maybe impossible), but I trust it will be a worthwhile journey for both of us. So lets take a walk.

Before we move to the beginning any further, there are a couple of words that are open to much misunderstanding, misinterpretation, and misdefinition. One is the term *church*, and the other is *kingdom of God*. These two concepts are replete in the New Testament documents, and I want to be certain that and I, and my reader, at least understand are on the same wavelength before we hopefully clarify the terminology of these two concepts. Because of this often-confusing use of these two words I am going to

Preface

deliberately use alternative terms, maybe extravagantly, so that my readers understand my usage of these terms.

For *kingdom of God* I am going to primarily use the alternative synonym *New Creation*, capitalized. I do this because *kingdom of God* is a concept that was rich in meaning to the Jewish tradition, to which much of the New Testament was written, but which is not at all meaningful to those who are not familiar with the Jewish culture. *New Creation* is a synonym that the apostle Paul used to refer to the same huge eschatological purpose of God to create all things new, and for that *New Creation* to invade this present age with God's design for the age to come. Know that every time I use *New Creation* I am referring to kingdom of God, and every time I use kingdom of God I am speaking to God's *New Creation*, which has been inaugurated in and through Jesus Christ. This concept appears in such other concepts as *eternal life*, *salvation*, and sometimes *righteousness*, but all speak of the same thrilling *New Creation* inaugurated in and by Jesus Christ.

Likewise, know that when I use the term *church* I am using the synonym *New Humanity* to refer to the community, or colony, and relational expression of the *New Creation*. Whenever I use the term *church* you will know that I am speaking of the *New Humanity*, and whenever I use the term *New Humanity* I am speaking of the *church*, or the reconciled human community that is the human and relational community resulting from the *New Creation*. Both of these terms speak of God's ultimate or *eschatological* design to make all things new. Make sense?

I hope that that clarification is not too confusing to my readers . . . but stick with me, and let's plunge in. It will, hopefully, become clearer with each emerging chapter.

— 1 —

WHAT ON EARTH IS THE CHURCH?

So I keep running across those young friends of mine who in our casual conversations ask me this very question: "*What on earth is the church?*" So that's the question before us.

What I will attempt will be to seek something of an adequate answer to that question, now asked more and more frequently by my younger conversation partners . . . those who are *not* the products of Christendom[1] culture. I love their questions. They are

---

1. Christendom can be defined as the period of history that began about the time that the Roman emperor Constantine made his newly found Christian faith the official religion of the Roman Empire. In a sense he co-opted the faith to make it useful for his purposes. He gave it all kinds of privileges and endowments, so that it would be comparable to the pagan religions that had been dominant—such as temples, a priesthood, rites, and political privilege. In essence, the church and the empire were on the same page, or became identified with each other. That comes down to us today with the "God bless America" response of officials, or the church's tax-exempt status. In Christendom the empire said to the church, "You pray for and support us, and we'll take care of you." There are a whole lot of inner contradictions and embarrassing episodes resulting from that Christendom concept, but the Christendom era is now rapidly fading, and our own culture is in transition into a post-Christendom reality, which is new territory for the church. That is presuppositional, and I will be coming back to it.

insistent questions asked in all honest curiosity and innocence, and they deserve some kind of helpful response.

One really needs a robust sense of humor, however, in engaging such an endeavor since the church is always an "in process" community, and often full of apparent contradictions. It is never perfect. It is made up of such diverse, and often unlikely, encouraging and discouraging pieces, sometimes wonderfully expressive of Christ's teachings. It is also made up all kinds of persons, sometimes fractured, sometimes eccentric . . . but also of many remarkable folk whose lives are beautiful living demonstrations of the new life found in Jesus Christ . . . and they come from every ethnic entity. The church's history contains so many mixed signals, which is why I purpose in these pages to help inquirers know what the church *is* and also what it *is not*.

To all of that let me add an introductory *caveat* here: The *church*, as it is set forth in the New Testament narrative, is ultimately *not a humanly explainable entity*. The church is created by the supernatural working of God's Spirit, or (if you can handle it), by the same Spirit that raised Jesus from the dead, and is now at work in ordinary human beings—for which working there is no category in the minds of most. Such a category doesn't even register on the scope of human rationality. To say that the church is both *complex* and *ambiguous* is something of an understatement—but the more one studies the history of the Christian church, the more one is inescapably forced to such a conclusion.

Then again, our answers will not come without sorting through and discerning all kinds of obfuscating and often confusing stimuli and misinterpretations along the way. So let me begin.

An Interesting Encounter Is a Good Place to Begin

I was having supper recently at a favorite village restaurant when I encountered a fascinating younger guy who is a gifted journalist by profession. He related how he had experienced a very moving moment recently when he and his wife, as tourists, had visited a famous monastery in Spain to observe evening prayers by the

What on Earth is the Church?

monks. His apparent lament was that (as he put it) he had long since abandoned the dogmatic Christian faith of his youth, and had accepted an agnostic view in the intervening years . . . but somehow listening to those monks chant the liturgy that evening stirred up within him something of a longing for a more fulfilling spirituality than was met by his own agnostic and intellectual explanation for anything transcendent. That encounter and discussion were very revealing to me of what is true for so many.

Driving home after my supper and that encounter, out of the archives of my memory came the words of a plaintive old negro spiritual: "Sometimes I feel like a *motherless child*. Sometimes I feel like a *motherless child*. Sometimes I feel like a *motherless child* a long way from home" . . . with its haunting sense of some incompleteness in one's life, something absent, something that is not as it should be. Something of that experience is what motivates me as I attempt to relate what I see to be the purpose of the church as it is intended to be in the design of God, and how, if it is true to its calling, it also speaks to the longings of all of the *motherless children* out there—all those seeking and curious inquirers who have that aching void in their subconsciousness, which all of the distractions of their social media culture cannot fill. This *inquirer's guide* is for those motherless ones, both those who are incredibly gifted and those who are fractured, hopeless, and confused—who have so much potential, but are also so lonely of heart. I long for them.

Why is there, deep within the human psyche, that quest for meaning . . . for some center to one's life, some authority, some creative source, some guiding line, some hope or final goal beyond itself? Why is there that quest after some fulfilling spirituality, that longing for true and caring relationships in our human journey? And why is there so much crap, so much brokenness, so much indifference to others, and such inhumanity expressed everywhere? Where do all of those questions and longings come from? What do I do with them? When all is quiet, is there some deep sense that I am really like a *motherless child*?

All one has to do is to read back over human history to realize that such thoughts and emotions are not at all new. Some have engaged in denial, and accepted their own self-determination that they are on their own to make the best of it, and not try to look for (what they contemptuously call) some cowardly and escapist *God-prop* out there somewhere.[2] Maybe Eastern mysticism? Or Zen Buddhism? Maybe New Ageism? Then there are those who engage in priding themselves in creating their own "designer gods," i.e., gods after their own making, in order to justify their "spirituality."

There are also the many who deliberately attempt to bury such questions lest the answers themselves might open possibilities with which they are trying to escape, and with which they don't want to deal. One can be ever so successful, so connected socially, and with such access through the Internet, with so much more information than any previous generation, so continually entertained . . . and still there comes out of nowhere those sobering moments when those haunting questions arise: "What is my life all about? Is there anything beyond this life? How would I know?" There are those who assume that joining some religious organization (like a church) will at least put them on good terms with whatever divine being there might be out there, and so they "cover their bases" with that affiliation.[3]

Atheism is also a "faith position" that simply refuses to accept that there is any God-being out there—period and paragraph—and is continually coming up with attempted answers to ultimate questions. *Agnosticism* may be a convenient escape, but it is not ultimately a satisfying answer. One of course can simply accept that we live in a context of chaos, without any metaphysical being who might be an ultimate source. We may reflect that this world is

---

2. A good record of this is the autobiography of C. S. Lewis, *Surprised by Joy*. Lewis was, unquestionably, one of the giant Christian voices and intellects of the twentieth century, yet he was a renowned agnostic in his early career, and a faculty member at Oxford University. He is poignant in his description of how God finally captured his mind and heart. Lewis is currently known more for his children's stories, The Chronicles of Narnia, but was prolific in his writings concerning the very quest that I am addressing here.

3. Alas, sadly, the church itself is inhabited by all too many poor lost souls, who become insufferably religious in their attempt to please whatever God there may be out there. The biblical narrative describes such as "having the appearance of godliness but denying its power" (2 Tim 3:5).

pretty screwed up, but then all of us are swimming around in some boundless, bottomless sea of chance . . . so "What the hell! Make the best of it!"

All of those are actually "faith positions." They are the assumptions upon which we build our lives. All of that points us back to the original question: What on earth is the church? Suppose that I were willing to acknowledge the possibility that I might be one of those *motherless children* and that I were looking for answers. Where in the world would I look? What in the world would I be looking for? How would I recognize it?

Such questions take us to the next surprising passage of our inquiry here.

— 2 —

WHERE YOU WOULD PROBABLY NOT LOOK

Unless a person were in some kind of desperation mode in seeking to find out where to look for the answers to those questions we just visited, and especially if one had a streak of skepticism or cynicism in himself or herself—and were resolved that we are all lost in the cosmos—one would probably *not* look at an eccentric peasant figure from a small city in a remote nation in the Near East who appeared quietly on the scene in the first century, making such utterly outrageous statements about who he ultimately was and why he had come onto the scene. Yet, that obscure beginning and unlikely figure is full or surprises.

Look again. Take a long hard look. Look again at the questions for which we are seeking answers, and then tune in to what that peasant was teaching and to why he was taken so seriously by those who encountered him, and why they were so constrained by what he was saying . . . as to become curious and begin to find him compelling, authentic, and utterly other than any of the ostensible religious leaders they had become accustomed to ignoring. Then take a long hard look at the awesome global impact that such an unlikely person has had over the ensuing two millennia of human history, and ask yourself: "*Am I missing something here?*"

Where You Would Probably Not Look

Take note: When the Creator God wanted to communicate his unimaginably great and ineffable love for his rebellious creation, his motherless children (persons such as you and I), he did not send a disembodied sermon, or a philosophical treatise, or some mystical experience . . . but what he did was literally come himself right into our human history. He came in the flesh-and-blood person of his Son, the one called Jesus. Yes, and this God-made-flesh-and-blood is this same eccentric peasant figure in that remote nation. Yes, but keep going: God's communication in flesh and blood is then assigned by Jesus to those who would become his followers as their mission, just as God the Father had given him his own mission. Those who make up the community of Jesus' followers are called by him "the church." The *church*, then, first of all, is to be that *present communal incarnation of Christ*, that same agent communicating the love and design of God for humankind, what with all of the mystery and wonder of such a community. Getting more confused? Stick with me.

When we ask, "What on earth is the church?," the answer is that it begins with that very Jewish person, that unlikely person: Jesus from the village of Nazareth in Palestine, which marginal nation was an occupied Roman colony. Yet, there had been an expectation within the Jewish community that had come down over many centuries, and especially from the prophet Isaiah in the eighth century BCE . . . that it was God's irresistible intention to *create all things new* at some point in the future. The Jews had mistakenly conceived of that prophecy with some vision of a grandiose world power that would overthrow Israel's enemies. God, however, had something entirely different and far more cosmic in mind than that common reductionist version conceived by much of the Jewish nation.

Take note, then, that Jesus not only came into the scene of the Roman Empire's militarily enforced *Pax Romana*, but he also came into the scene of the powerful religious establishment of Judaism, with its long and well-documented history. That religious establishment was focused in its temple in Jerusalem. The priestly hierarchy of the temple was the dominant cultural influence in

Palestine, notwithstanding the presence of occupying Roman legions.

The *church* we are seeking to understand here is not even remotely understandable apart from the person of Jesus, his teachings, and what he accomplished historically through his life, then his tragic death . . . and then by his powerful resurrection from the dead. That resurrection, witnessed by multitudes, is what was the confirmation and explanation of all that he had taught those who followed him. All of that took place in the cultural context of the Roman occupation, and the dominance of Judaism, and the temple in Jerusalem, into which Jesus made his appearance.

Around that fact of Jesus there came into being a whole new and different kind of human community, a humanly unexplainable community, which *communally* demonstrated Jesus' teachings in its lifestyle, in its relationships, but also in its irrepressible enthusiasm and conviction about the privilege of communicating to others the teachings of Jesus. Jesus' teachings were about himself, about who he was, and about why he had come among them. But even more, they gave answer to those questions that lurk in human hearts, in the hearts of all the *motherless children*. It was, therefore, also a community actually mandated by Jesus to communicate all of that to all of those others of the human community who could also be designated as *motherless children*.

Yet, look again! You will find, as have innumerable multitudes of others such as yourself over these past two millennia, that this Jesus is the one who demonstrates the love of the Creator for his stubborn and rebellious creation. Or to take a bit of literary liberty, Jesus the Son is also the divine *Mother* seeking her *motherless children*. Or in the terms of the narratives of Jesus' life and teachings, Jesus is the Father God taking on flesh and blood and coming to search out, find, and rescue those very real persons who are lost, and who long for their heart's true home—like you and I. Jesus is the infinite and unimaginable love of God for such as we. This is the absolute and unalterable foundation of the church, and its necessary cornerstone, which is necessary to the understanding in our quest for an answer to the question, "What on earth is the church?"

Where You Would Probably Not Look

We will need to look at how the church took shape, but I want to leap over to near the end of Jesus' earthly career, when he asked those who had been his intimates, his disciples, for many months, "who do you say that I am?" (Matt 16:15). Upon their amazed recognition that he really was the long-awaited *Messiah*, he then made the rather enigmatic promise to them that it was upon that messianic reality—that *eschatological* reality of his own central role as God's anointed in the midst of human history—that he would build his church. We need to tag that statement, because it is one of the only places that Jesus uses the word *church*, and he says that he himself would build that church! *He did not commission his disciples to build the church.* He would himself irresistibly build his church. That is often a point of confusion. What we need to file away here, however, is the fact that his messianic mission would also find form in *colonies* of the *New Creation*, of his *New Humanity*. The message would have visibility in communities of those whom he would call by their announcing and demonstrating the gospel of the kingdom of God—the gospel of his *New Creation*.

But then, he never gave them any kind of a blueprint of how he would do that! Oh? But if you stop and look, he already had! His only commission to them at the end of his earthly life, after his crucifixion and resurrection, was the plan: "*All authority in heaven and on earth has been given to me. Go therefore and make disciples of all nations, baptizing them in the name of the Father and of the Son and of the Holy Spirit, teaching them to observe all that I have commanded you. And behold, I am with you always, to the end of the age*" (Matt 28:18–20). Do you see the difference? *He* would build his church, but *they* were to make disciples—both part of the same ultimate mission.

A couple of critical pieces need to be observed here. First, he did not instruct them to go and found new religious societies or institutions. Society was surfeited with many religious societies and sects, with their temples and rites. Rather, he told them to "go and make disciples" (we'll come back to that). But secondly, and near the end of his earthly presence, he also gave them their long-range strategy, or game plan, which was: "*And this gospel of the kingdom will be proclaimed throughout the whole world as a testimony to all nations, and then the end will come"* (Matt 24:14).

Now try to compute those two: From an isolated, marginal band of his disciples, to the heralding of an upside-down gospel of the kingdom of God that was unlike anything else, to every people group on earth without any institutional form of their message... and this all to be done by making disciples. Say what? What did that mean? What was their model?

To my inquirers, let me explain that for at least the last millennium and a half, since the intrusion of the "Christendom Era," the church's theologians have constructed a theology of the church that primarily sought to define the church in an institutional forms, but they have also have essentially started their studies from the post-Pentecost apostolic teachings of the early church, rather than with Jesus' own demonstration of church formation through his time with his disciples, from their calling to the consummation of all things. I want to challenge their procedure in developing an understanding of the church. Jesus had taught his disciples that the gospel of the kingdom of God was like leaven, and would grow spontaneously and irresistibly, and so permeate its setting, wherever. I also happen to believe that Jesus had been demonstrating, or illustrating, how this *church* was to be his building of his *New Humanity* communities through a one-on-one discipline, which would later be designated as *disciple making*. It all began from the moment he came out of the desert after his baptism. Jesus began to build his church from that very beginning of his ministry in Palestine.

Here's the background: Jesus was a Jew, and the Jewish community had a long history that is well documented in one of the oldest written narratives in human history—that narrative actually goes back into prehistory, and to the very beginnings of the human community, and was passed down by oral tradition until it began to be recorded in written documents sometime in the second millennia before the Christian Era. In that history there was always a *metanarrative*: namely, that the God who created the world, and against whom early humans declared their autonomy

Where You Would Probably Not Look

in a primordial act of rebellion, always had a plan to ultimately to reconcile it to himself and to make it all new—to recreate it. That's a study in itself. Enough to say here that there was an expectation recorded in that written narrative of one who would come and put it all to rights (called, in the Hebrew language, *Messiah*, or "Anointed One"), to inaugurate a *New Creation* (or the kingdom of God), to give answer to the mystery of human history (give answer to our questions!), to display the infinite love of the Creator God for his own creation, and so to reconcile the world to himself—to God—which somehow would involve his own death on a cross (the mystery of the cross is a study in itself) in order to justify humankind's very real guilt (because of its rebellion and attempt at autonomy) and bring us again into the Father God's intimate embrace.[1]

That was the expectation that was part of the Jewish heritage, and that was always sort of "out there" in the mind of the Jewish community. Jesus' own birth itself had been remarkable, and those who were eyewitnesses of that birth related it to that Jewish expectation of a Messiah (or Christ). We do, in fact, have a record of its drama from eyewitnesses who were present. Jesus was born exactly where the ancient prophets said the Messiah would be born. It is all of the events surrounding that birth that are annually celebrated to this day in the Christmas story by the community of Christ's people (but, alas!, currently celebrated more by the commercial interests in the marketplace than the church).

The birth was unique—miraculous in fact. The parents of Jesus were ordinary godly peasant folk, bewildered by all that surrounded his birth, such as Mary's virgin conception. But the only other reference to Jesus' early life we have is that at the age of twelve he was taken to the temple in Jerusalem for Passover, and he amazed the priests with his knowledge of their scriptures—all of

---

1. The term *gospel*, which was used to designate Christ and his message, was a common Greek word that conveyed some kind of a super-thrilling announcement. It could be used of a military victory, or of any event that was enormously meaningful. So Jesus' followers adopted it to refer to the thrilling news of the inbreaking New Creation, or of sins forgiven, or of Jesus himself. That word comes to us in English as *gospel*.

which says worlds for the ministry of his parents in teaching him the Hebrew traditions in their home.

After that, Jesus disappears for a couple of decades, until he emerges quietly and without fanfare in a remote wilderness scene where his eccentric cousin (who was known as John the Baptizer) was calling the Jewish folk to get ready for the immanent coming of their long-awaited Messiah. John was doing that preaching out in the boondocks, and multitudes of expectant and serious and pious Jewish folk went out to listen to his message, and to receive a baptism of repentance by him, and so to get their hearts ready for the coming of their long-awaited Messiah.

Out of his years of silence, living in the village of Nazareth, Jesus turned up at that wilderness scene, unannounced, and requested the baptism John was offering. In so doing Jesus was identifying himself with his people Israel (for whom he was the representative, but that also is a study in itself). John became unmistakably aware at that moment that this cousin of his, this Jesus, son of Mary and Joseph, was actually the very one about whom he had been unknowingly preaching . . . and because of that awareness John was reluctant to baptize him, protesting that Jesus ought to be baptizing him instead. Jesus insisted, however, and so John responded and baptized him. John then reported that he saw the Spirit of God descending upon Jesus in a bodily form like a dove, and that he heard a voice from heaven saying, "This my beloved Son, with whom I am well pleased" (Matt 3:17). John the Baptizer recognized what he was witnessing, but apparently few if any others did. (John would soon be arrested for making the paranoid King Herod the object of some rather severe prophetic preaching, and would ultimately be beheaded).

Jesus departed from that scene of his baptism to then spend forty days in solitude and fasting in preparation for his God-given mission, and for his entry onto the public scene. There he was isolated and alone to be challenged by the diabolical figure of Satan, who would use all of his seductive wiles in order to tempt Jesus to seek an easier way to accomplish his mission—some way that would avoid the necessity of the *cross*. (This again is a study in

Where You Would Probably Not Look

itself: Satan, the arch-enemy of God, evidently realizing the potential for his own downfall if in fact Jesus carried out the necessity of the cross. The mystery of the cross is that it is the actual *key* to God reconciling the whole creation unto himself—again, a thrilling study in itself.)

Then, in what is almost an understatement, the earliest written witness about Jesus simply states: "Now after John was arrested, Jesus came into Galilee, proclaiming the gospel of God, and saying, 'The time is fulfilled, and the kingdom of God is at hand; repent and believe in the gospel'" (Mark 1:14–15). With utter candor he announced that in himself God's New Creation was being inaugurated—and for our interest here, that such a New Creation would include a New Humanity. That New Humanity would begin immediately. The narrative reports that one day John the Baptist (before he was arrested) pointed out Jesus to two of his own disciples, and said to them, "Behold, the Lamb of God, who takes away the sins of the world!" (John 1:29).

Those two then, out of curiosity about what such a dramatic statement meant, left John the Baptist and sought out Jesus. Right after that is our beginning: Jesus turned and asked them what they were seeking. They responded, addressing him as Teacher, by asking him where he was staying. His response is classic *disciple making*: "Why don't you come and see?" So they spent the rest of the day with him. Here is our beginning core of Jesus building his church, since Jesus right at that point essentially *calls out* those two . . . and the leavening (and church building) begins. One of them then went and found his brother, and brought him to Jesus by telling him that he had found the Messiah. There then follows the story of Jesus building this initial community, as one by one the number began to grow, and that small community of Jesus' followers spent time with him, and he began to form them by his teachings, and to take them along as interns on his public ministry of teaching and healing.

The very *sine qua non* of the church, and of its mission, begins with one's encounter with Jesus, and with the intellectual and moral decisions to become his follower and to be formed and transformed by his teachings. Not only so, but as the number of disciples grew, Jesus focused himself on just twelve of them, in a very unique and intimate relationship, in order to reproduce himself in them. That illustrates a basic form of the church: a small enough fellowship (or colony) that all of them know and all are responsible for each other. Even after Jesus' ascension into heaven, and after Pentecost, when there were thousands who had responded to the message of Christ, they met in public for teaching, yes . . . but then they were also together in homes and around the table eating, processing the apostle's teachings about Jesus, and investing themselves in each other in costly love, i.e., they were visible colonies of God's *New Humanity* in Christ.

Bring Your Questions and Look and Listen

There is not a single shred of grandiosity in Jesus' appearance on the stage of history. He didn't even have any identification with the accepted religious establishment of Judaism, which was centered in Jerusalem and with the temple establishment. Moreover, they were quite suspicious of, if not downright threatened by, him.

Backtracking just a bit and rehearsing Jesus arrival on the public scene: Coming, as he did, from his time of testing in the wilderness, he went first of all to his own home synagogue in Nazareth, where everyone would know him as a local boy, and there he was given the privilege of reading the scripture for the day. That particular scripture was a messianic prophecy from Isaiah that prophesied that the Messiah would be one endowed by the Lord's Spirit, and would preach good news to the poor, recovering of sight to the blind, and liberty to the oppressed, and proclaim the great year of Jubilee.

Then Jesus did something totally unexpected and audaciously unthinkable for a local boy. After he had read the prophecy, he rolled up the scroll and gave it back to the attendant. If that were all that he did, it would probably not be noteworthy. But it is what he said next that was both his inaugural statement and was that which enraged the familiar folk of Nazareth: "Today this scripture

Where You Would Probably Not Look

has been fulfilled in you hearing" (Luke 4:21). They went ballistic. They even tried to kill him. This was a local boy. They knew him. Who was did he think he was, assuming that he was God's Messiah? How unforgivably arrogant!

Then, however, Jesus actually began to do those very messianic works, such as healing the sick, casting out demons, feeding the hungry . . . but always preaching the thrilling news of God's New Age, God's *New Creation*, God's *New Humanity*, God's in-breaking new kingdom, which was actually being inaugurated with and through his own presence among them.

Please take note again that Jesus didn't come to establish some new religion. Those Palestinian Jews had religion aplenty. Jesus didn't even hang out with religious folk, or with the temple crowd. Rather, he made himself available, speaking and teaching quietly, on the back roads of Palestine, sitting in rural places or socializing with those who were probably considered profane and irreligious. The Jewish folk had no category for a Messiah who would make his appearance in such humility. Jesus was building his *church*, and doing it in an almost hidden method (which method is continually forgotten by too many ecclesiastical empire builders today). Along the way he would make outlandish statements such as: "Whoever has seen me has seen the Father [God]" (John 14:9). "I am the way, and the truth, and the life" (John 14:6). "I am the door. If anyone enters by me, he will be saved" (John 10:9). "I am the resurrection and the life. Whoever believes in me, though he die, yet shall he live, and everyone who lives and believes in me shall never die" (John 11:25). "Come unto me, all you who labor and are heavy laden, and I will give you rest" (Matt 11:28).

Listen: Doesn't that sound like someone who just might understand those questions that lurk in the hearts of the *motherless children*—their quests for meaning, for acceptance, for hope, for some guiding line in their lives?

So there were those (at first cautious folk) who began to take notice of such a person as Jesus, and to listen to what he said, and to watch what he did. They were a '"mixed bag" of different types of personalities. They don't appear to be those who were necessarily reflective philosophically or theologically. They certainly were not anything like some first-century flower children looking for some new spiritual trip. He never hid the fact that to follow him had a definite cost, and dangers. They were simply ordinary folk making the best of each day of their often-difficult lives. They were folk such as profane fishermen and shady public figures, a disparate mix of personalities (even a future betrayer) who were made curious by what he was teaching and doing, and so began to follow him to see what he was all about, and to wonder what it all meant. And the longer they were with him, the more they were captivated by him. It is such as these who give us our first clue as to what we might be looking for in our own quest.

What on earth is the church? Note here that it all begins with Jesus' calling, or with his inviting of individual persons with names and faces and stories (persons just such as you and me) to come be with him, and to be formed by his teachings and his company. The *church* is a people called to a Person who would open to them a whole new reality, which he identified as the *kingdom of God* (or as I choose to translate it, the *New Creation*). Jesus began to attract a new community of those who saw in him someone who could answer the lurking and profound questions with which they all lived. More and more people began to listen and to follow, and consequently the fascinating word about this person and his teaching spread rather quickly . . . but (take note) Jesus selected only twelve out of a much larger number of his followers to be his intimates. There was obviously a sizeable group of others, including some marvelous women who ministered to him.

I would repeat for my readers that we need to take special note of that select group of twelve, because it speaks to a basic dynamic in the formation of the future church,[2] and that is that the *basic unit of the church* must be small enough for there to be true intimacy, for strong *one-another* relationships, along with mutual-

---

2. There are, to be sure, those who will protest that the number twelve reflects a fulfillment of the twelve tribes of Israel, which may be true . . . but more immediately he wanted a number with whom he could be in regular intimate dialogue, and whom he could be forming into the leadership for that *New Creation* community he was, in fact, building by his Spirit.

Where You Would Probably Not Look

ity, true accountability to each other, and genuine responsibility for each other. It is commonly acknowledged among those who study group dynamics that twelve to fifteen is the optimum size for healthy working units.[3] There can be much larger gatherings for instruction and celebration, but Jesus modeled this basic reality in his choice of the twelve. Keep that in mind as we proceed on this walk and observe Jesus building his church.

The question comes naturally: Why in the world would those guys leave what they were currently doing, disrupting their ordinary lives, and begin following this Jesus into such uncertainty . . . unless they found in him something so inexplicably compelling, so authentic and explanatory, so convincing and revealing, and from him found answers to the profound questions they harbored in their hearts? There would have to have been a compelling conviction that he was, possibly and actually, who he was stating that he was—that he had in fact actually come from his Father God and was doing the works of his Father, and that God's *New Creation* was on the doorstep. He was either true or he wasn't. Jesus was saying something that was so radically different from what is commonly and ordinarily taught by many religionists: God is not sitting in splendid isolation awaiting folk worthy of his acceptance. Quite the opposite. Rather, in Jesus, God has invaded his own human community in the flesh-and-blood person of Jesus, in order to seek out and to save those who are his lost children. *"God so loved the world . . ."*

Again, you *motherless children*, please take note: What you have before you is Jesus calling out men and women to recognize what God was saying in and through him—that he was the expression of God's love for the world, and that they, as they came to him, would find true life, be set free, be made new, and henceforth be formed into the community of his *New Creation*. You're looking at the emergence of the *church* in the world. The whole foundation

---

3. Dunbar's Rule insist that 150 is the largest number of persons with which one can have any kind of meaningful relationship at all, but the smaller range of 12–15 defines recreated intimacy and love between persons with names, faces, and stories.

and meaning of that church is to be found in the person of Jesus Christ. Jesus is, as one early follower would say, "the mystery hidden for ages and generations but now revealed to his saints" (Col 1:26). Jesus gets bigger the longer you look at him.

To be sure, he spent many months wandering the back roads of Palestine teaching them, feeding the hungry, healing the sick, even raising the dead, but then he also taught them that it was necessary for him to ultimately to be killed, or crucified, and that such was essential to his mission—which his followers could not at that time comprehend. He answered their questions and doubts. He sent them out on training missions, and then called them back and refined them. All the while, those followers, those disciples, struggled to comprehend that part of his teaching about the necessity of his death, and were even more confused when he assured that after he had been killed he would rise again from the dead. Those predictions of his passion and resurrection simply didn't register with them; they had no category for such a notion, and it wouldn't be understood until after it had all actually happened.

The church is incomprehensible apart from its passionate focus on Jesus . . . and upon his death on the cross, and his resurrection.

We revisit, then, that dramatic moment in the final days of his time with them, in the days immediately before his crucifixion. He was with them in the city of Caesarea Philippi, and he asked them, "Who do people say that the Son of Man is?" They then reported several possibilities that had been suggested. Then he asked the Twelve point-blank, "But who do *you* say that I am?" Peter became the spokesperson for the Twelve and answered, "You are the Christ, the Son of the living God." Jesus then blessed Peter, and made a statement that demands our absolute attention in our quest in this book and about what follows. Jesus affirmed Peter's answer (and made plain that it had been given to Peter by the Father in heaven) . . . but then Jesus stated that it would be "on this rock," or that *messianic* foundation, that he would build his church, and that—this enigmatic statement—"the gates of hell shall not prevail against it" (Matt 16:13–18). Somehow, that indicates that the church will not be built without a conspiracy of the forces of darkness always seeking to prevent it from happening (we'll come back to that later).

What all of that means for our pursuit here is, first off, that the church is not to be formed by our own human initiative, but also that it comes into being by the calling of Christ to men and women that they should come to him, and in him find not only their heart's true home, but the power of a new life. That calling also comes in multiple and often-unexpected ways that somehow catch our attention and require further inquiry. It further affirms that the church is Christ's building, so that even when its human participants "screw it all up" and do it wrongly, and get distracted or immunized or derailed . . . Jesus will do what is necessary to continue the building until it is complete.

That said, let me conclude this section of our quest by quoting an essential principle in our understanding of the essence of the church. It is a principle by one of the first generation of the church's most eloquent and influential teachers, one named Paul: *"For no one can lay a foundation other than that which is laid, which is Jesus Christ"* (1 Cor 3:11). So that when you ask where to look to understand what it all means, and what life is all about . . . the answer is that you ought to be able to look for that colony or community of folk who are formed by their mutual and passionate embrace of Jesus Christ, and by their decision to be faithful to his teachings and to engaged in his mission. Such colonies may be as small as two or three, but are demonstrative of *New Creation*. That mission also requires that they express his own selfless love to one another within the community.

Knowing that such a discovery may be easier said than done, and that there are some obscuring factors that need surfacing, some realities that may be only very marginal, let me next do something of a full disclosure, and confess that the existential church, which we encounter in our quest, can be most complex and ambiguous—and, yes, frustrating and off-putting at times. At the same time, it has been awesome in its history and influence in innumerable lives, not mention creating a whole new culture that has accomplished unimaginable blessings globally over the past two millennia. I will attempt to help you next to understand something of the landscape.

— 3 —

JESUS THE ROCK: HIS MESSIANIC MESSAGE AND MISSION

This chapter is perhaps a bit unusual, but it is necessary, and here's why: I was having a delightful conversation over supper one night with a friend whose whole life had been lived without any conscious contact with any of the Christian stuff, like the Bible, church jargon, Jesus, and all of that. She had grown up in something of a totally secular, or New Age, culture, and was pretty resistant to what she knew of the Christian thing. She was, however, intrigued by my "weird" faith in Jesus, and how that formed my life. She was herself always into a quest for *spirituality*, but without much of a sense of how that was achieved—but always trying. In our conversation that evening she would occasionally stop me in my tracks and say, "What does that mean?" That all made me conscious of how I communicate to a set of *post-Christian* inquirers. I may not succeed, but I will attempt here, then, to do some collating and paraphrasing in order to communicate an answer to the question, "*What on earth is the church?*". . . to just such folk as this friend. If you already know all of this, then skip over this chapter and move on to the next. Okay?

So, here are those twelve guys who had now spent something like, maybe, two years in the company of Jesus as he moved all over that small nation, and even across its boundary into Syria on occasion. They had watched him. They had listened to him. They had been sent out by him on intern missions, and then called back to him and refined. They had become a community—something of a model of what the true church should be—a small community bonded to Jesus and to each other in a mutual life of love for him and for one another as they engaged in his mission. At the climactic period of Jesus' earthly presence with them, they were together in the northern district of Caesarea Philippi (Matt 16:13ff.) when he dropped the big question on them, "Who do people say that I am?" They then reported back all of the various rumors and appraisals of him they had heard.

"*But who do you say that I am?*," he asked them directly in return. That's the critical question. Had those intimate disciples of Jesus gotten the point of their many months in his company? Peter, the spokesman, reported, "You are the Messiah/Christ, the Son of the living God." Jesus blessed Peter for his answer, and then gave a bit of an enigmatic answer, which is loaded with implications for our quest here. At that answer from Peter, Jesus said, "Absolutely. So may your name be Peter [the Greek word here, *petros*, means rock], but this answer has not come to you by your native intellect. It has been revealed to you by my Father in heaven . . . but *upon this rock I will build my church*, and the gates of hell will not prevail against it" (paraphrasing Matt 16:15–18).

In so many words, Jesus was saying to this initial community of his intimate followers:

> Okay, guys. Yes! I, even I, am in fact the long-expected *Messiah*. Yes, and it is upon this rock that I am going to *call out* a whole new human community, a *New Humanity*, a community expressive of the *New Creation* that I have come to inaugurate . . . and it will be irresistible. I am the one who will be building it. Yes, but you also are a critical piece of this mission. As the Father has sent me, so am I sending you. What you have seen and heard and learned from me, you will now put into practice as my

disciple makers. When men and women respond to your message, you are to baptize them, and carefully instruct them in all the things that I have taught and commanded you. In so doing you will be my faithful witnesses, and I will be calling out and building my church through you. In this way, there will be formed spontaneous colonies of my *New Humanity*, ultimately, to the ends of the earth, and within every ethnic group.

In so many words, but in an unmistakable way, he was saying to them:

> Whenever you pray, "Your kingdom come on earth as it is in heaven," you will be reminded that the *age to come* has now invaded *this present age*, and that it is the determinative reality from this point on. And rest assured that I am with you even until it all consummates at the end of the age. Only one more thing is lacking for you . . . and that is that this is not a merely human enterprise, but requires the dynamic energizing of the Holy Spirit, whom I will send.

Something like that.

What the disciples didn't get yet was the necessity of his crucifixion and resurrection in order to accomplish his reconciling mission, what with their lingering vision of some kind of a grand and temporal dominion. Their eyes would be opened only after the fact of his resurrection. Only then would they, and the whole New Creation community, be able to testify, "God forbid that we should glory, save in the cross of Jesus Christ or Lord."

Jesus wasn't engaging in riddles or playing games with them; he was asking them to embrace the very essence of what he had been teaching them and demonstrating to them over those past months: who he is, what is his message, and what they are to do with it. If one conscientiously wants to know *what on earth is the church* . . . then that person has to base his or her understanding on three unmistakable dimensions of what Jesus' life and ministry had been all about: 1) Jesus as the *Messiah*; 2) Jesus' *message* about himself as that *Messiah* and about the inbreaking kingdom of God, his *New Creation*, which he was inaugurating; and 3) his *mission* to incarnate the love and grace of God for his whole creation, and for the whole lost and rebellious human community . . . through the *church*.

Everything is about Jesus, and about God's design to reconcile the world unto himself. Everything is about God so loving the world that he would give his Son so that all may become partakers of that love and so be formed into the likeness of God's Son.[1] That's the purpose of Christ's *called-out* community.

The Rock: Jesus the Messiah

Jesus was unequivocal about his identity as the Son of the living God. He would declare that he was the one sent by the Father in fulfillment of God's promise of an *Anointed One*, a *Messiah*, to bring deliverance and healing, to make all things new, and to inaugurate God's *New Creation* . . . as well as to forgive sins and set men and women free, and so to reconcile his lost and rebellious and confused sons and daughters to himself at an inestimable cost to himself: his death on a cross. Jesus also laid claim for himself the venerable name of Israel's God, which is the name *Yahweh*, which God had given to himself when asked who he was (which means something like, "I am that I am"). Jesus would periodically describe himself by saying (in the Greek), "I, even I, am the way," or, "I, even I, am the bread of life"—a subtle but telling reference to the fact that to have seen him was to have seen *Yahweh* of Israel,

---

1. For a couple of extravagant sources in the New Testament narratives, try Romans 8:28–30 about being called for the purpose of being conformed to the image of God's Son, then justified and glorified. If that's not enough, try 2 Peter 1:3–4, which tells of God power whose purpose in Christ is to make us partakers of the divine nature. Nothing miserly about that.

Jesus the Rock: His Messianic Message and Mission

the *I Am That I Am God*. When asked at his own trial if he was the Messiah, Jesus responded, tellingly, "*I am*" (Mark 16:61–62).

The *church* is, first of all then, all about Jesus the *Messiah*. Human language really doesn't "carry the freight" of such a reality ... that the Creator God has come in the person of his Son to put all things to rights, to shatter the cosmic darkness, and to deal with the guilt and condemnation out of his infinite love and grace for his creation.

When that reality is displaced or forgotten, the *church* ceases to be the church in any authentic sense. What on earth is the church? It is that new community *called out* by Jesus Christ and inhabited by those who have embraced Jesus Christ as God's Messiah. The church always begins by persons responding to Jesus' invitation, "*Come to me, all who labor and are heavy laden*"; "*I am the door . . . I came that they may have life and have it abundantly*" (Matt 11:28; John 10:9).

The Rock and the Message

From the very day that Jesus began his teaching ministry, he "came into Galilee, proclaiming the gospel of God, and saying, 'The time is fulfilled, and the kingdom of God is at hand; repent and believe the gospel'" (Mark 1:14–15). That is the consistent theme. Its reality and centrality is designated in other ways, with such concepts as *salvation, eternal life, New Creation, forgiveness of sins,* etc. But it is the reality that in Jesus Christ the *age to come* has invaded this present age and is *now* the dominant reality in this world. At the very end of his time with his disciples, Jesus would prognosticate that " *this gospel of the kingdom will be proclaimed throughout the whole world as a testimony to all nations, and then the end will come*" (Matt 24:14).

Everything that Jesus did and taught relates to that reality. His healings and miracles reflect the power of his kingdom. His feeding of multitudes speaks to prophecies about the God feeding the hungry in the kingdom. His great *Sermon on the Mount* in Matthew's account, or *Sermon on the Plain* in Luke's account, spell out the lifestyle of that kingdom. The kingdom of God has its center in Jesus Christ. The kingdom of God creates a whole new lifestyle of righteousness. The kingdom of God calls forth the spontaneous and contagious readiness to be messengers of peace. The promises of the gospel kingdom of God are our shield against accusations that come from the darkness. The kingdom of God produces a whole new way of thinking that is called "the mind of Christ." The gospel of the kingdom is our message, and its communication is our passion. And yes, the gospel of the kingdom of God gives us access to God through prayer, since we are, none of us, sufficient by our merely natural resources.[2]

The message of Jesus is the church's authority and guiding line. God's people operate on a whole different wavelength, a totally different understanding, than those who are formed by this present age. That message is very earthly and practical. "They kingdom come on earth" is not at all "otherworldly," nor is it divorced from the tragic realities of this human scene, or from God's passion to create all things new.

The disciples had heard Jesus teaching all of that, and displaying it in his mighty deeds. Within a couple of decades they had recorded it all for our benefit in the New Testament documents. What on earth is the church? It is the community formed by the teachings of Jesus and the apostles, and inhabited by those who have embraced Jesus as the one who is who he says he is, and so have found in him the power of a whole new life.

The Rock and the Mission

Jesus did not call his disciples (and he certainly does not call us) to be passive and isolated from his own passion to seek and to save the *motherless children* of this world. His word to his disciples, and to us, is, "*As the Father has sent me, even so I am sending you*"

2. These seven components are the seven pieces of the Christian's *whole armor* listed in Ephesians 6.

JESUS THE ROCK: HIS MESSIANIC MESSAGE AND MISSION

(John 20:21). When he told them that upon the rock of his message and mission he would build his church, that should not have seemed to be such a strange word to them, since he had actually been demonstrating to them for those many months the dynamics of calling and forming a whole new human community through his invitation and his teachings. When his followers embrace Jesus by faith, they thereby become part of who Jesus is—they come to abide in him and he comes to abide in them—and therefore become a dynamic part of his mission. A person cannot be an authentic follower of Jesus and be indifferent to those other very real persons whom Jesus came to call back to their heart's true home . . . or be indifferent to this groaning creation waiting for God's recreating work.

What on earth is the church? It is a people such as we who today incarnate God's love for the world, and for the very real and often really screwed-up people who live around us, and for the groaning world around us, with all of its seemingly intractable difficulties. "As the Father has sent me, even so I am sending you"—not in theory, but in actual engagement. The church is a whole colony of such *New Humanity* persons employed by Jesus in his very real mission to be the *light of the world*.

— 4 —

WHAT ON EARTH ARE YOU LOOKING FOR? (AND WHAT ARE YOU NOT?)

So, let's just assume that as an *inquirer* you have become persuaded that all that we have just been speaking of concerning Jesus is exactly what your subliminal longings have yearned for, and that he is actually the one who brings to the world meaning and acceptance and hope . . . and so much more. And let's assume that, what with all of the sketchiness of your understanding of him, you have responded to him as a person, and have cast your lot with him in an act of trust. You may have done this in some encounter with his teachings in writing (maybe this book), or maybe you have encountered him in a person, or persons, who are his present day followers, or those who believe in him. You may also understand from our previous discussions here that, somehow, as Jesus came to inaugurate his kingdom, his *New Creation* . . . that New Creation also inevitably produces a *New Humanity*, and that there are colonies of that New Humanity actually existing right here in this present scene.

That still leaves us with our original question: *What on earth is the church?* Who makes up the church? What does it look like? Where would you find it? How would you discern its authenticity

What on Earth Are You Looking For?

over against all of the hustlers of religion that turn up everywhere? The second question, then, would be: What are you *not* looking for? A bit of a reality check may be in order to insert right here: The church is made up of the full spectrum of persons, all the way from the fickle, fractured, and disappointing, to the diverse, enormously gifted, and encouraging . . . and all in between—just so there are not too many surprises on your quest! But also remember that all of this new community is still always in process of being formed into the image of Christ. It is never complete, always provisional, but it is always Christ's building.

First of all, by way of orientation to what I will ultimately propose as four visible markers of the church, as are unmistakably taught by Jesus and his apostles, let me confuse you a bit more and say that the church is a *mystery* that defies merely human explanation. We modern and Western folk are always looking for neat, black-and-white, rational definitions . . . and that doesn't work for the church. When a respected Jewish leader approached Jesus one night, he wanted some kind of a theological explanation of what Jesus was teaching. Jesus answered with a metaphor, or maybe a riddle, saying to that inquirer, whose name was Nicodemus, that he must accept the fact that there is a whole other dimension of reality into which he needed to be born, namely, the reality of God's Spirit, which is like a wind that blows, and the evidences of that wind can be seen, but not the wind itself. So, Jesus explained to Nicodemus, are those who are born of the Spirit.

The church is like that. The church is the creation of God's Spirit, God's calling, God's working, and it comes into being in unexpected ways and unexpected places. At the same time, it exhibits a key component of God's *New Creation*, in that God has not created humankind to be alone, but has created in humankind the need for community, for family, for relationships grounded in mutual love. That can be one other believer, or two or three, or maybe a dozen or so . . . but the working of the Spirit reconciles the human community with a kind of depth and genuineness that is so critical to God's purpose for us and the world.

In the world today, the largest expression of the church is undoubtedly (would you believe?) house churches, or small, often clandestine gatherings of those who have embraced (and been embraced by) Jesus Christ. You cannot trap the church within an institution. It is mysterious and contagious, and it is the several components that make it visible to the world that we need now to pursue.

It is also necessary for me to remind our inquirers that God, by his Spirit, is the dynamic factor in a person discovering Jesus Christ, and that same Jesus has given to those who embrace him the gift of communication with him, with his Father in heaven, and that gift is *prayer*. So, supposing you have become persuaded of Christ by yourself, how then do you discover the church? You do what multitudes in the most unlikely and difficult and hopeless places in the world have done over all of these generations: you pray and ask for some contact with those other believers in Christ . . . and don't be surprised where you might find them.

Since it is God who is at work in us, and who is in us, and for us, through Jesus Christ, then know that your response to Christ's calling makes you a very real part of the church that he himself is building. Christ is the one who calls, and Christ is the *Door*. He invites us in, but he doesn't invite us into any merely human religious society; rather, he invites into that community which is his dwelling place by the Holy Spirit. That ought to get our attention!

Here, at least, are four visible dimensions of Christ's *New Humanity* colonies that give us clues: 1) the *New Creation* community's passionate *focus on the centrality Jesus Christ* in all that he came to be and to do; 2) the *New Creation* community's *embrace of Christ's mission* in this very real world as being its own mission; 3) the *New Creation* community's *relationships of love* as expressive of the Father's relationship to Jesus; and 4) the *New Creation* community's demonstration through its *lifestyle*, which is redemptive, often radical, and produces life and hope and joy. The teachings of the New Testament are replete with these four components. So let me unpack them a bit more, so that in your quest they may be in a bit clearer focus.

Focus on the Centrality of Christ

Jesus was not dispassionate in his love for the church, for which he gave his life. It was his mission from the Father to reconcile the human community, and to bring it back into the embrace of the Trinitarian community, free from guilt and alienation, and with all of the prerogatives of the family of God—yet there was an infinite cost in his accomplishing that mission. It is that huge theme that also produces the metaphorical description of the church as the "Bride of Christ" or the "beautiful bride for the Lamb of God." That means that the inner dynamic of the church is always that it is being recreated into intimacy with Jesus Christ, and that as such it is being so conformed to his likeness, so adoring of him, so obedient to his commands . . . that at the consummation of all things it can be presented to Christ as a bride "without spot or wrinkle" (Eph 5:27). That is the design for the mission of God in sending Christ into the world. The church is always to have the *sweet aroma of Christ* (see 2 Cor 2:15) about it—and is even now in process of being formed into such.

To be sure, the church is to be a community of caring, of intimacy, where we are responsible to each other and for each other . . . but behind it all is the fact that Christ lives in us and he becomes the church's sure Foundation. That being so, we look for that colony that does not relegate Christ to any secondary reason for its life together. We are called to be *Christ* to one another. Our passion and focus is Jesus Christ. Have I made that primary enough?

Intentional Embrace of the Mission of God

Authentic colonies or communities of God's *New Creation* in Christ are never passive about their calling to be engaged with him in his cosmic "search and rescue mission," which is inseparable from his dwelling in and among his people. Jesus never called his *New Creation* communities to be composed of passive hangers-on, or those who see the mission of God as somebody else's responsibility. Jesus' quest to seek and to save the *lost* becomes the passion of every one in whom he lives. Such colonies or communities (because Christ lives within their daily human lives) are also to demonstrate God's own unimaginable love for this very real (most often problematic and fractured) world of men and women—for the whole human community. God's people in Christ are to be the *heralds of God's invitation to such as we enter into his reconciling grace.*

It is to be a community consumed with passion for Jesus Christ (his life, teachings, death on the cross, and resurrection) and eager for that reason for all to know him. It is the communal expression of seeking God in the here and now of the very real and existential neighborhoods of our experience. The same God who sent his Son to make known his grace and love also *sends his church*, his *New Creation* colonies, to make that grace and love known to all with whom they come into contact, and among whom they dwell (not with religious arrogance or superiority or insensitivity, but with gentleness, humility, and love). God sends his *New Creation* folk, his colonies of his *New Humanity* (the church), to call the *motherless children* back into the divine embrace and acceptance. To that end Jesus sends those whom he *calls out*, individually and communally, back into the heart of the human scene as *"the missionary arm of the Holy Trinity."*[1]

Jesus, in some of his final instructions to his followers before his crucifixion, said, *"As the Father has sent me, even so I am sending you"* (John 20:21). That is the communal mandate, namely, that those who make up the church are to be looking for those who are still sensing the incompleteness and emptiness of their lives, and so to call them out of their inner darkness and into God's marvelous light and freedom . . . and no one is exempt from that mission. Any community claiming to be a church but is ingrown, or spiritually ossified or incestuous, or indifferent to those whom

---

1. As beautifully expressed by some of the Christian teachers in Latin America.

Jesus came to seek and to save, is a contradiction, and is a "church" that denies its very calling.

Now, to state the obvious: those first two evidences become obviously empty unless those very colonies demonstrate the tangible realities in their relationships with one another, and in their lifestyle.

The Lifestyle of the New Creation Community

What the watching world observes with somewhat critical eyes is how those who profess to be Christ's followers *behave*, that is, how they live out their purported New Humanity incarnation. Face it: this is a very reasonable requirement on their part. When those who profess to be the citizens of God's inbreaking kingdom actually live out his teachings, then that may well incite curiosity and inquiry from the world. The converse is also true. When those who live lives that contradict the teachings of Christ and of the apostles, then that can call forth all of the cynicism and negativity of onlookers. Colonies of God's New Humanity in Christ demonstrate that very New Humanity in their lifestyle, and that is a whole-life proposition. It is not confined to some categories of religion or spirituality; rather, it involves the totality of our lives, and of the world in which we live: socially, culturally, intellectually, politically, environmentally (what with all the dimensions of humanitarian engagement, economically, domestically—the whole of life.)

Jesus taught that as men and women live out his teachings (such as those succinctly taught in his Sermon on the Mount) onlookers will see their good works—their New Creation lives—and know that somehow God is the source of such unique lives . . . lives that are *salt and light* in this screwed-up human scene. In such lives the love and justice and design of God for the human community become visible to observers. That is something that our *inquirers* will need to be looking for in their quest to know what on earth is the church.

In observing the lifestyle of such followers of Christ, those onlookers (those *motherless children*) will see communities in any one of numerous sizes and forms and makeups, which seem to have a radically different *inertial guidance system*, or creative source, along with their understanding of the realities of daily life. Such people's thinking and behavior is formed by Christ and his teachings. Again, it is the *aroma of Christ* that surrounds the most modest of God's people, the church, and that gives it good degree of authenticity.

The Relationships within Colonies of God's New Humanity

Right at the formative stage of Jesus' time with his disciples he stated, "*As the Father has loved me, so have I loved you*" (John 15:9). "*A new commandment I give to you, that you love one another: just as I have loved you, you also are to love one another*" (John 13:34). The common human quest for warm, authentic, caring, and reconciling relationships should find flesh-and-blood demonstration in such colonies. That is costly love. It is reconciling love. It is forgiving love. It loves not only those who return love, but even enemies and those who despitefully use it. Such relationships of self-giving love do not overlook wrongs or injustices or prejudices, but it loves redemptively and with reconciling grace. Such love can never be depersonalized or merely theoretical or formal. It depends on knowing the object of one's love, and being willing to spend energy, emotions, and possessions—whatever it takes—to demonstrate that. From the very beginning of the church it was that demonstration of *New Creation* relationships that caught the attention of so many in the Roman Empire.[2]

Those four demonstrations might be considered something of an *algorithm* in one's quest to discern what is and what is not the church. But along the way there may be some factors that emerge that may confuse the inquirer.

---

2. Readers may want to check out the *Letter to Diognetus*, available many places online.

Some Factors You May Find Confusing

I enter this subject with some trepidation, because I am in a sense challenging a couple of centuries of tradition, and it is always hazardous to one's health to challenge tradition. (There was a day when one could get burned at the stake by the church for challenging its venerable traditions.) There are good traditions, and then there are those that totally distract the church from its message and mission. Full disclosure: I am a product of several of the factors I will list in what follows. And the picture is never black or white. Within most of the several factors that I will list, there exist viable colonies of God's *New Creation* people—churches (colonies of *New Humanity* folk) within "churches"—seeking to faithfully live out their calling. At the same time, in my conversations with friends in the emerging generation, these puzzling phenomena come up and elicit some skeptical questions, as well they should.

First of all, let's talk about *Christendom*. That designation pertains to a bit of history that did a good job of subverting the church from its essence as a community of *aliens and exiles*, a community that does not dwell in human temples, but whose being is determined by its mutual life together in the adoration of and obedience to Jesus and his teachings. For its first several centuries the church was essentially faithful to that self-understanding, and it remained a mobile, versatile, flexible—even elastic—missionary community. That was also a period of regular horrific persecution and discrimination against the church by the Roman Empire.

One can only imagine that, after all of that suffering and deprivation, notwithstanding growing into a major culture-creating reality within the empire, it would be quite seductive when the Roman Emperor Constantine professed to be converted to Christ and put his blessing on the church . . . and then was insistent on providing it with all of the accouterments of the pagan religions, such as status and security, a professional priesthood, sanctuaries, liturgies, etc. The Christian church soon found itself to be the official religion of the empire. The empire had effectively co-opted the church. That was about the worst thing that could have happened to it . . . but then we have lived with this *Christendom* reality now for two millennia. Much of what follows is the result of that cultural conformity, so unwittingly accepted by most until recent times. We are now rapidly moving into the *post-Christendom* era, if in fact we are not already there (but that's a whole study in itself).

Then there are *denominations*. Our inquirers are not basically looking for some church with a denominational label, even though one might discover such colonies within such. Denominations have all kinds of derivations. Many will claim to be the one true church. But one of the earliest Christian affirmations of faith, the Nicene Creed, declares that the church is: *one* (no matter how many expressions), *holy* (uniquely and intimately related to God through Christ), *catholic* (universal, encompassing all of humankind), and *apostolic* (always guided and self-correcting by the teachings of Christ and the apostles). There are the vast ancient church hierarchies, such as the Roman Catholic Church, and the Greek Orthodox, and Russian Orthodox, and Coptic churches, which date themselves to the early centuries of the church as an attempt to establish their order and orthodoxy, but which have often become wealthy and powerful and controlling and controversial . . . but then show signs as smoldering embers of life burst into flame within them.

There are the Protestant churches, which arose out of protests against the aberrations and abuses of the more powerful church entities. Some came into being around the person of a strong and influential teacher, while some came into being because of a particular doctrinal emphasis. Some were just obstreperous groups who had a difficult time cooperating with anybody but their own kind. Then there arose, in more recent times, the *Pentecostal* denominations, which were focused on the person and work of the Holy Spirit. Yes, and probably most of all, there would also be the vast and uncontrollable number of independent churches who are the fruit of the passion to fulfill Christ's commission.

To be candid, much of what professes to be "the church" may not be such at all. When one looks at our *algorithm* (or whatever) above, there are a lot of strange communities that one finds it difficult to define as colonies of God's design in *New Creation*. At the same time, again, one may find dwelling in such denominational congregations those smaller colonies of persons consciously called by Christ. Someone designated such colonies as "*ecclesiola in ecclesia*," or "little churches within the church."

Another confusing concept is the *church defined as a place or a sanctuary*. A church is a community or a colony, not a place. With the event of Christendom, or whatever provoked that move, the church moved backward into the understanding that there are *sacralized* places, which were (and are) mistakenly called "the house of God," suggesting that such a place is where the church is. It became, therefore, the design of missionary church planters to build a *place*, or a *sanctuary*, so that believers could "go to church," not realizing that believers are the church wherever they are, wherever they meet together. Granted, this *church-as-place* misconception has called forth some magnificent bits of artistic and architectural genius... but such places are not the church—though again, colonies of God's *New Humanity* may, and often do, find some lodging within such. Still, the mission of the church nowhere allows for the notion that the church is to create sacralized buildings. So when you're looking for the church, you may never find it in "church buildings" with signboards out front, alas!

Then there are *clergy and church professionals*. Since I am one who has worn that designation for sixty years, this is dangerous for me to approach. But again there is no such category ever mentioned in the New Testament documents. There are mature and proven and wise leaders mentioned, but they emerge from within the community, and they understand their role as that of equipping and overseeing the people of God into maturity, and into fruitful engagement in the mission of God. Still, the church, unfortunately, has a tendency revert to merely "human religion." There are those who aspire to be called "Reverend" or "Doctor" and yet have never proven themselves in the community as its gifted leaders. At the same time, there are many (and I trust that I have been one such) who have sought to create vital colonies and make disciples. When you are looking for what on earth the church is, you may want to look at how its ostensible leaders incarnate the four dimensions of our *algorithm*. Those don't come automatically with an academic degree in divinity.

Next (however charitable one desires to be) there is that phenomenon of *unconverted leadership*, as much as that may sound like an oxymoron. However, the reality is that there are more than a few of those who have emerged into church leadership out of an inner need to be important, or to serve humanity, who themselves have never encountered Jesus Christ. That also explains what comes next. You may want to ask whatever clergy person you encounter to tell you his or her story of faith in Jesus Christ. If they are embarrassed at your inquiry, they may have answered your request already!

And yes, there are *unconverted church members*. Those are the persons who are attracted to the church society for many reasons, but have never been converted through intentional repentance into faith in Jesus Christ. One very significant Christian leader called such persona *"religious Christians."*[3] My observation is that much of the church is a vast mission field, and much of my career has been evangelizing church members. That can be most disconcerting for an inquirer who is excited about his or her newfound relationship to Jesus Christ. I don't want to pursue this subject further, just to tag it as a potentially confusing phenomenon.

We could multiply such stumbling blocks, such as the church's different expressions in different cultures, or church communities that are indifferent to the neighborhoods (geographical, professional, social, etc. neighborhoods) in which they reside. Or there are the institutional churches whose gospel is themselves, or what I call *ecclesiocentric churches*, which proliferate in-house activities to keep the faithful happily occupied with attractive *churchified* involvements, but not the mission of God.

---

3. See Dietrich Bonhoeffer, *The Cost of Discipleship* (New York: Macmillan, 1937).

Before I close this chapter, I really do *not* want to emphasize the negatives, but rather to ask my inquirers to go back to the beginning and rehearse those things that one *should* look for in discerning colonies of God's New Creation, knowing that you will find them in unexpected places and forms, composed of those who have, like yourself, encountered Jesus and who take him and his teachings seriously, and joyfully, in their daily occupations.

— 5 —

THE DOOR AND THE DISCIPLINES

What on earth is the church? Our basic answer to that question has been that the church is intended to be the very visible communal expression of the *New Humanity* that God has inaugurated through Jesus Christ, his Son, which, of course, makes it a community that is inescapably focused on Jesus himself. That communal expression becomes visible in the four dimensions that are incarnated in the colonies of that *New Humanity* as those who embrace Christ by faith begin to have his life formed in them so that their lives begin to reflect him and his life. That life, then, becomes visible to inquirers, and to the watching world, at least in those four dimensions that we looked at in the previous chapter, and which we termed something of an *algorithm* for our quest. (We also took note of several factors that are potentially distracting or obfuscating factors that might confuse us.) So back to the basic premise: that the church on earth consists of those communities in process of being recreated into God's design.

Still, that leaves us with several more questions whose answers we need to have clearly in our minds:

1. Where is the door into this *New Humanity*?
2. How does one find it?

3. What's on the other side of the door? And . . .
4. Is one willing to accept the consequences of entering into anything that is so unknown and so awesome as such a *New Humanity*?

Where Is the Door?

This is what Jesus is all about. He himself is the *Door* into God's New Creation, and consequently into the community of God's *New Humanity*. Jesus makes this claim for himself: "*I am the door. If anyone enters by me, he will be saved and will go in and out and find pasture*" (John 10:9). That metaphor is given in the context of Jesus presenting himself as the "good shepherd" who calls his sheep by name, and who provides for the most profound needs of his sheep (his followers). Similarly, in his invitation to those seeking understanding into the most profound mystery of life, Jesus makes himself the door into that discovery: "*I am the way, and the truth, and the life. No one comes to the Father except through me*" (John 14:6). Jesus' continual invitation to those encountering him and his teachings is always, "*Come unto me . . . and I will give you rest*" (Matt 11:28).

The simplest answer to knowing where is the Door into the community of God's New Humanity is . . . that the Door is Jesus, who is God's *Anointed One* sent to inaugurate the recreation of all things and to reconcile us to God. The Door is not some set of spiritual disciplines, or joining some ostensible church institution. The Door is entered by persons, such as you or I, embracing Jesus as being precisely who he says that he is: the Door who is the only way into our heart's true home. It is looking at all of his promises and claims and saying, "Yes! I embrace that. I receive you into my life."

There is also the accompanying question as to how one finds the Door.

How Does One Find the Door?

In a sense we have already answered that question, but then again maybe we have not. If Jesus Christ was raised from the dead by the Spirit of God . . . then somehow he is alive and present in this very world in which we live. Jesus had a very difficult time convincing his disciples of an alternative narrative to their misconceptions of what his kingdom would be. They still had some notion that is was something that it would be within their power to bring into being. That misconception made them incapable of realizing that the reality of his kingdom, his *New Creation*, was one quite beyond their human capacity at that point to conceive. He insisted that the task that he was giving them was not at all humanly achievable, and that they must wait upon the coming of his Spirit. That didn't register with them either. They kept questioning him about his kingdom (*New Creation*) as though it were just an updated version of the kind of merely human religious establishment that they knew. It wasn't until after his crucifixion, after his resurrection, and then after the dramatic events at Pentecost[1] that they saw what he had been saying to them, and were then able to realize that the church was now the dwelling place of God by the Spirit—that only by the Spirit could men and women be turned from darkness to light, and have their eyes opened to such unbelievable New Creation.

The dynamic presence of the Spirit became the energizing force of that *New Humanity* which Jesus inaugurated. One of the results of that dynamic presence was that the apostles were constrained to write down an accurate record of not only all that Jesus was and taught, but also of the mission of the church in that first generation under their guidance as Christ's apostles. That written

---

1. The Jewish feast of Pentecost took place fifty days after their Passover observance. It was during this Pentecost observance, after the crucifixion and resurrection of Jesus, that the great watershed event took place when the Holy Spirit descended upon Christ's followers, and the message of Jesus was heralded with great power to the astonished gathering from many nations. In a sense, the church and its witness became public in this event, which could only be described as awesomely supernatural. From that moment the word of Jesus went everywhere, and has not ceased to this day.

The Door and the Disciplines

record is our New Testament, and is the authority and guiding line for the church. That book is also a powerful witness in its own right, and it is that introduction to the Door that is powerful far beyond any rational explanation. How does one find the Door?

The first answer to the place of discovery might well then be that very book we call the New Testament.[2] But then also, as simple as it sounds, the second and most obvious answer is that the Door is discovered through those real persons whom we encounter who have already entered through the Door. We discover the Door by one-on-one conversation with those who have already discovered the Door, entered it, and found new life. The good news of Jesus and his *New Creation* over these two millennia has spread through the contagious lives and conversations of those who have entered the Door, who have experienced Christ living in them and setting them free, and beginning the process of recreating them into the divine image. Such New Creation lives are to incarnate warm, sensitive, good-humored, caring conversations . . . in daily routines, over the back fence, over coffee or beer, in casual and sometimes weird settings.

The answer, however, is not limited to these two primary means of discovering the Door. There is a mysterious *force field* at work in the world, which also includes dreams, miracles, visions, healings, and other evidences of Christ's passion in his cosmic *search and rescue mission*. (The fact that you are still reading this raises the likelihood that you are already, somehow, caught up in the *force field* of the Spirit of God, since God is not at all passive in his love for you and for the human community. There is that mysterious and ineffable *Wind of God*—the Spirit of God—by which Jesus Christ is creating his *New Humanity*, his church. Does that sound weird? It is! Where does spiritual hunger come from? What provokes curiosity about such things? What, or who, opens people's eyes to things they have never seen before, or opens their

---

2. Just to note that the New Testament flows out of the promises and historical realities of the Jewish community recorded in the Old Testament. But that's a whole study in itself.

ears to hear things to which they have previously been deaf, or makes their hearts responsive to such?)

Then again, that *force field* does produce some interesting episodes that cause discovery of the Door. There is an account of a Berber in Islamic North Africa who, upon reading the very positive things spoken about the prophet *Isa* (Jesus) in the *Qur'an* and becoming curious, then pursued that curiosity about *Isa* into resultant faith and trust, and so experienced a whole new life in Christ, which he lives out joyfully and sensitively in the midst of that not-usually-congenial Islamic culture.

Or there are those illegal Latin American immigrants in a prison in the Pacific Northwest who, through some unique Bible studies by a gifted missioner,[3] are being set free in their lives, and are experiencing forgiveness and healings and joyous new life, even though they are still imprisoned and often guilty of crimes.

There was a much-publicized account a few years back of a very highly placed government lawyer who was convicted of engaging illegal activities, was sentenced to prison, and disbarred. But just before his imprisonment, in his broken and shattered life, in desperation he visited an old friend, a wealthy corporate executive but also a follower of Christ, on a Sunday evening. That executive quietly proposed to this broken man that he consider Christ, and by his own account of this challenge states that before he was even out of the driveway of that estate he burst into tears, called out to Christ, and his life was transformed by this Jesus whom he barely knew. Yes, crisis moments, when life caves in, are often the provocation that points those broken person to the Door.

The mystery of the *force field* of the Spirit has been a source of wonder for all of these centuries. In recent times in such an oppressive nation as China, where followers of Christ have been sentenced to concentration camps (especially during their cultural revolution), it has been those very concentration camps that have become remarkable generators of new life in Christ for those who were prisoners there, because in those prisons the followers of

---

3. See Bob Ekblad, *Reading the Bible with the Damned* (Louisville: Westminster John Knox, 2005) for an account of this ministry.

The Door and the Disciplines

Christ did not have to be clandestine about their witness to Jesus anymore, and so their caring lives were contagious. Concentration camps became equipping centers for that vast network of underground churches in China.

The *force field* was at work in Latin America, where there was an acute shortage of Roman Catholic priests, and so the *campesinos* in remote villages were somewhat on their own for long periods between the visits of the priests. It was when they attained some basic literacy that they would gather in their meager homes together in the evening, after days of grueling work, to read and ponder and discuss the accounts of Jesus, and to reflect on the meaning of Jesus for their own difficult lives. Out of those gatherings emerged base communities of faith, and those primitive base communities became generators of a contagious and faithful discipleship, and pointed thousands to the Door, so much so that their regional Roman Catholic bishops hardly knew how to cope with such awakened communities that had developed apart from their priestly authority. Those base communities also became a transformational social force. How do you account for that?

Or consider the account given to me recently by an eyewitness about a very remote nomadic village in Siberia whose village leader, on one of his long snowmobile trips to the nearest town for provisions, heard rumors of a teacher there who was proclaiming Jesus, and around whom all kinds of good results and hope and joy were being generated. The village leader asked if someone could come to his encampment and tell the others about this Jesus. My eyewitness reported to me that within three days of the arrival of the Christian teacher nearly the whole village had been baptized, and a church had been formed because the *mighty Wind of God* had been at work in those nomadic tepees bringing life and hope to old and young.

Another account came through missionaries in the mid-twentieth century about their approach to a very remote, presumably hostile, and primitive tribe in Indonesia for the first time. What they found astounded them. Instead of hostility they found, rather, that among those ostensible head hunters there was actually a longstanding expectation, from a vision generations earlier, that their hope was in their waiting for *a white man with a book* who would come. That vision had passed down through generations, so that when the missionaries arrived they were received with joy, and the tribe embraced Christ. Dreams, visions, miracles, and healings are also part of the *force field*.

All of these illustrations are to say that one never knows where or how one might encounter the one who professes to be the Way, the Truth, and the Life. The New Testament Gospels are replete with Jesus's invitation that such spiritually hungry and thirsty persons should come unto him: "*Come unto me . . . and I will give you rest*" (Matt 11:28). There is also the promise that, "*to all who did receive him, who believed in his name, he gave the right to become children of God*" (John 1:12).

Multiply this "ten thousand times ten thousand"[4] over these two millennia since Jesus walked the earth, and it should catch the attention of even the most cynical. Yes, the church being created by such a *force field*, by such a mighty Wind of God, is a great mystery . . . and for one to get close to it has often unexpected implications.

What's on the Other Side of the Door?

Yet, any inquirer will ultimately need to come to Jesus, who stated, "*I am the door. If anyone enters by me, he will be saved*" (John 10:9). At the same time, I am assuming that my inquiring reader may have a bit of a cynical streak in himself or herself, and, having been hustled by a whole lot of false advertising in his or her life, will immediately ask, "Door into *what*? If Jesus is the *Door*, what is on the other side? What are the consequences? How am I to know? I'm not about to jump before I look!"

Those are incredibly wonderful and necessary questions, because Jesus is never even a tiny bit deceptive about the cost or following him, or the cost of being his followers. Yes, and Jesus also knows, in his love for each unique person, that we humans all

---

4. In reference to the hymn of this title by Henry Alford.

The Door and the Disciplines

bring a lot of "luggage" with us that we will need to get rid of if we are to be set free and to know the "freedom of the glory of the children of God" (Rom 8:21). There is indeed a cost to discipleship, and that is never veiled in Jesus' teachings . . . but accepting that cost is what enables his sons and daughters to be building upon his solid foundation. Jesus, for example, painting another of his word pictures, told that the path to his new life requires that those who would enter it must forsake the broad and popular road in that it goes nowhere but to destruction . . . but that the road to his true life requires that one must enter a way that is hard, and go through a gate that is narrow, i.e., get rid of a lot of hindering luggage.

That is why the invitation (or challenge) that Jesus always delivers, in conjunction with his preaching of the kingdom of God, is prefaced with the command to *repent*, i.e., to have a transformation of mind—in short, to forsake all of their attempted *autonomy*, their efforts to be their own gods and goddesses. The prerequisite for having Jesus come into our lives with his own life is that we acknowledge that all that we bring to him is our need of him. That is the threshold of the second part of his invitation, which is to embrace the thrilling news of all that he has come to do in us and in the world—in his *New Creation*. We cast ourselves on his reconciling and recreative love and grace, and do so with the confidence that somehow all of our hope and our true life is to be found in such a relationship to this welcoming Savior.

Jesus is the entry point of our heart's true home.

But there is a surprise on the other side of that Door. When we embrace Jesus by faith, and take up our residence in him, and when he and his Father—as he promises—also then take up their residence within us . . . guess what? His life in us then is then irresistibly drawn to all of those others in whom he dwells—Christ in you and me is the same as Christ who dwells in all the others who have passed through the Door. This is the beginning of the colonies of the *New Humanity* that continually emerge along the way. It is such bonding between Christ in you and Christ in me that creates a whole *New Humanity*, wherein we are enabled to love God with all of our hearts, and love one another as we love ourselves. This is the *in-process* human community that is being recreated into God's original design for his humanity, far beyond what we could ever ask or imagine.

We're talking about the *church*! We are looking at what is the source of those four dimensions, four demonstrations, of our *algorithm* that make the gospel and the church visible to the world. We become Christ to one another, energized by the same Spirit. We can never again be indifferent or seek anonymity in such a colony.

Is One Willing to Accept the Consequences?

The cost of discipleship—the cost of coming through the Door—is that we do not escape this present scene. We are not taken immediately into heaven, or into some never-never land of pleasant spiritual experiences, but we become the presence of Jesus Christ in the very existential scene that is our daily context. In a very real sense, we become the answer to the Lord's Prayer. We are those who are called "to his own *glory and excellence*" and are made "*partakers of the divine nature*" (2 Pet 1:3–4), with all the joyous fulfillment and risks of that calling. God's name is exalted, his kingdom comes, and his will is done through real human beings who become the *Body of Christ* today in the midst of the human scene, the agents of his inbreaking kingdom, his *New Creation*. This is such a compelling calling that those who are called are quite willing to deny themselves and follow Christ even unto death.

Those who pass through the Door and into God's *New Humanity* then form themselves into colonies. These colonies, small enough to be intimate and caring of one another, small enough to bear each others burdens . . . then they become support and encouragement and nurture to one another in their mutual sojourn as aliens and exiles. The colonies mutually "*teach and admonish one another in all wisdom, singing psalms and hymns and spiritual songs*" (Col 3:16) in the midst of the vicissitudes of each passage of their sojourn. It is those colonies who hold us accountable, and for whom we are responsible. Different times and circumstances mean that the colonies are not permanent, but change with circumstances and locations and require different forms, but they are always Christ to each other in the changing scenes of our pilgrimage as Christ's disciples, and his visible demonstrations of the *New Creation* before the watching world. In the transient present neighborhoods, and what with all of its networks of social media and digital connections, there are all kinds of new and challenging dimensions of creating such colonies.

Such colonies don't happen by accident, but require equipping disciplines, and so one finds that in healthy colonies those more mature practitioners of this new life, who then become the mentors and the models for those newly through the Door. Each of those new followers needs to be equipped in the Word of Christ, equipped in the understanding of their cultural context, along with their missionary responsibility to be reproductive, and also equipped with the capacity to be wholesome and sensitive communicators of the message. Each is to be equipped in the disciplines necessary for their daily ministry of being God's *New Humanity* in Christ in whatever set of circumstances they find themselves.

There are, to be sure, always those attempts by the relentless darkness to divert the church from this calling, but those "gates of hell shall not prevail" (Matt 16:18) against the church, which Christ calls into being, and we'll come back to that necessary understanding later on. Meanwhile, the church is breaking out into new expressions, and new dynamics, and with its focus on creating those disciples who are contagious and reproductive. This is a global phenomenon, and it emerges in multiple forms of colonies formed in and by Christ. Such colonies or communities are contagious with the thrill of what God has done in Christ. So, what on earth is the church? It is that new community that is being formed in and by and for Jesus Christ.

We need to move now to another expression of the church, which is that of being the context in which reconciled relationships and the practical love of God's New Creation are incarnated. To that end, let's move now to the form and the functions of such colonies.

— 6 —

THE CHURCH: ITS FORM AND FUNCTION

When a person hears the invitation of the Good Shepherd, "Come unto me!" and "I am the Door," and has responded and come into his sheepfold, then he or she then enters a whole different kind of human community, which is not like any other human community. When a person comes to Christ and enters into him, Jesus Christ also comes and enters into that person by his Word and by his own Spirit. What that means is that we become those with a new and divine DNA, or a different operating code (whether we feel anything or not), and so we are included in a community of others who also have that new life. They become part of a community of others who are also being formed into the image of the one who has called them, and it is that formation that begins to produce in them, individually and corporately, those four demonstrations of what we defined as an *algorithm* in an earlier chapter.

Such communities of God's *New Creation* (or communities of God's *New Humanity* in Christ) are not captive to any single form. Such communities of those whom Christ calls may take on any one of a myriad of forms. Those communities are the church. It is not their form that is our focus, but their function, which is the formation of God's image in his sons and daughters. The forms are very flexible and are continually reinventing themselves.[1] That said, we also are aware that such does not just happen. It must be an intentional communal formation. We do not enter the sheepfold of the Great Shepherd fully formed, and our formation is a lifelong process of having Christ in us as that dynamic reality that gives us authenticity as the Body of Christ in and to the world in which we live.

Earlier in our quest we noted that one of the tragedies of our lostness, our *motherless child* dilemma, is that there is that quest for autonomy that is so common to all humankind, and is quite isolating, and destructive of loving communities. Wherever or however that quest for autonomy is explained, or where it came from . . . it is also one of the pathologies that destroys true human relationships. It keeps cropping up even after we have come to Christ, and we must continually name it and renounce it in our coming. Such renunciation is called *repentance*. Thus it is that when we come to Christ, and he comes to indwell us and to incorporate us into his *New Humanity*, a primary discipline is the formation into true and wholesome and intimate and caring and loving relationships. Yes, and it is those relationships that are one of the four demonstrations that are visible to the watching world. Our new life in Christ is never anonymous, or impersonal, or passive, or private. We are actually commanded by Christ to love one another as he loved us, and it is by such demonstrable love that others will know that we belong to Christ.

A basic evidence of Christ living in us is *one-another love*. As a matter of fact, the *one another* principle in the New Testament teachings is basic to the description of the church.

With that in mind, and with our basic question, "What on earth is the church?" . . . we can know from Christ's teachings

---

1. One of the confusing factors of former and traditional paradigms, or patterns, of the church was something of an institutional rigidity, and of ecclesiastical control, which tended to ossify the church, and to immunize it to its missional purpose. Such patterns and paradigms may not have had much to do with actually being the demonstration of the New Humanity, or of its formation—or they may have actually been quite fruitful, for which fruitful expressions many of us are quite thankful.

The Church: Its Form and Function

that it is the church that he is building, and is somehow to be an expression of forgiving, serving, reconciling, caring, warm, and mutually encouraging relationships. This still doesn't get us to the answer we need. Let me say it again: We don't come into the Door equipped to immediately demonstrate such; some are more naturally equipped and less broken than others, but the love that the Spirit of God generates in us is a radical love, and a practical love that is not easily discouraged. Still, we need to learn to live out such relationships, and to do so in actual colonies or communities of our *New Humanity*. We certainly do not enter such colonies full-grown. And, we come with our diverse personalities that have the potential of irritating one another. It is not at all unusual to find in a community strong personalities along with weak ones, or fractured personalities along with those well disciplined, or some controlling and psychotic persons, or timid and withdrawn persons along with those gifted and good humored. We are all in process of being conformed to the image of Christ.

The question comes again, then: What is to be the *form* of these communities? And the answer is that the form is elastic, or that the church expresses itself in any one of multiple forms. If we learn anything from looking at the church's history since its inception by Christ, it is that the church is continually reinventing itself for different challenges, contexts, and times as it has moved from Jerusalem out into the whole world. The church emerges in quite different social, cultural, political, and economic contexts. It doesn't establish itself in permanent residences. Colonies of God's *New Humanity* are mobile, versatile, and flexible. The form of the church is not the focus. There have always been, and are, those attempts to trap the church into some form, or to codify it . . . but there is no blueprint for the form of the church. It is hugely complex and multiform. However, there are some patterns that do emerge, and that we will come to shortly.

One thing that must remain focal is that the *function* of the colony, in whatever form it may take, is that of equipping and encouraging one another into maturity in Christ, into fruitful and mutually ministering, into being truly human men and women who can authentically be called the "Body of Christ." These colonies become the demonstration of Christ to the watching world. Again, such a function must be somehow deliberate. There must be some discipline by which those coming through the Door as little children in the faith are then taught and encouraged into adulthood in the faith, and are able to do the same for others. Such a discipline cannot be "boilerplate" or "one size fits all." Each individual person is just that: a unique personality.

I keep close by me the small classic booklet *St. Benedict's Rule for Monasteries*, odd as that may sound. As the church moved out into an unfriendly world, it often did so through dedicated men and women who formed themselves into supportive residential presences for their ministries of teaching, or evangelizing, or caring for the humanitarian needs of the more helpless. That required vows of total dedication, and none were encouraged to enter such vows lightly. To that end, there was a progression offered to those on the margins who were curious about such communities. One might come initially as an *inquirer*, be given hospitality, allowed to investigate, ask questions, share in the daily life and disciplines, and to become oriented to the requirements, with the freedom either to walk away from it or to request to be accepted for the next stage.

The second stage was that of a *novice*, in which one, by request, was included into the community as a learner, taught the Scriptures, the daily disciplines, the servant role required, and assigned regular duties and oversight to see how one performed—something like that. If, after a period as a novice, a person desired entrance into the vows of the community, the others in the monastic chapter would vote to receive him or her and the applicant would take vows of obedience to the rule of the abbot and the community, and so become a *member* of the order.

That may sound a bit severe to our independence-minded modern person, but it at least is instructive that persons coming *de novo* through Christ the Door need to learn the disciplines of living in a whole new race of men and women in this world, to be the people of God in Christ . . . and so there needs to be a formation, or

The Church: Its Form and Function

a discipline to accomplish such. Right here I will acknowledge that such is all too rare. But I will also insist that this very discipline is what Jesus defined as *disciple making*, which he made the basic component of his missionary mandate to his church. The making of disciples, which included baptizing them into the vows of faith, was teaching them to *obey*, or observe and practice all that he had taught them. The end result of such was a mature, contagious, and reproductive community.

At this point we need a *reality check*. Such illustrations seem insanely unreal to our culture, which seemingly only knows how to relate over their smartphones, and so can easily escape whatever is demanding or uncomfortable to their own self-interest. But just stop and look at where we have been. Our inquirer has seen Christ in some other person(s), or found him in reading the New Testament, or become curious about the lifestyle or relationships of some acquaintances who are believers, and so has come through the Door and is now looking for some others with whom to share this new life, this discovery. What form would a colony or community take? I can only offer a few pointers. As we noted above, there is no blueprint here, but there are some patterns that emerge that help us to understand the relationship between the form of the church and the disciplines of its formation.

The first patterns come from Scripture itself. Jesus demonstrated them well. First of all, he did proclaim his message of the good news of the inbreaking kingdom of God to *large groups* of people. His public teaching was the primary means of getting his message out to the larger population. That's *pattern #1*. But then, as people heard his awesome message about the *New Creation* that he was inaugurating, and as some began to respond . . . he selected the Twelve to be with him—those would become his intimates, in whom he would reproduce himself, and to whom he would commit the mission. That's *pattern #2*. But there was also a somewhat larger and ambiguous group of his followers, numbering seventy and more, who were also part of mission, and that is *pattern #3*. He would appear with the Twelve, primarily, after his resurrection, and so fine-tune their understanding of what they were to do. At the same time, he also appeared to a much larger group on occasion to assure them and make them part of his post-resurrection mission. That much we learn from Jesus himself.

Our next pattern comes from the post-Pentecost church.[2] It is very difficult to form any kind of a rigid ecclesiastical pattern from the brief descriptions of those immediate chaotic days, except that again the several thousand who were dramatically converted by the Pentecost event met publicly (probably in the temple courts) for teaching by the apostles, but then the narrative adds that they were together in fellowship, in the breaking bread in their homes, sharing their lives and possessions, and praising God (Acts 2:42 ff.). That innocent-sounding word *fellowship* actually is a word loaded with implications, since it is from the Greek word *koinonia*, which carries all of the sense of an intimate, mutually caring, and unselfish love for the other persons within that *koinonia*. Institutional church traditionalists have tried to develop out of that "breaking of bread" a pattern that would make the breaking of bread into the formal eucharistic rite, as practiced in the traditional and formal rites of Christendom. The response to that is: yes and no. Jesus had, unmistakably, told his disciples in the upper room (as they celebrated the Passover feast before his crucifixion) that when they were together they should break the bread and drink the cup in remembrance of him. In the later epistles it is quite obvious that such a eucharistic meal was celebrated, but in that period of the church meeting in homes and sharing meals was apparently common practice.

It is difficult to conceive of the huge crowds of thousands meeting publicly after Pentecost and being able logistically to so celebrate the Eucharist. It must have, of necessity, been something of a mark, even an essential discipline, of the church since those

---

2. Pentecost, as we observed earlier, was the Jewish celebration that took place fifty days after the crucifixion of Christ, and after his resurrection, when the Holy Spirit came upon the infant church in such awesome power. It proved something of a watershed event at which time the church launched into its global mission, which continues to this day. So we refer to the next pattern as the *"post-Pentecost church."*

initial days, and this primarily because it was instituted by Christ himself.

Still, it is worth pausing here long enough to notice that the size of a church community can be very small, and that it does not require some church professional to preside at such eucharistic observances, but that the eucharistic celebration is to be a regularly observed, in its simplicity, and as a continual *re-evangelizing* component of the gatherings of God's people. It could and would be hosted by whoever would have been the acknowledged leader of those small gatherings meeting in homes.

Then there is the pattern of the form of the church provided by Paul himself. The record of his visit to the city of Ephesus is most instructive. Being a Jew, Paul as a traveler naturally found his way to the synagogue when he came to Ephesus. It was there that he initially told the assembled Jewish folk of what had happened in Jerusalem with Jesus—his crucifixion and resurrection. It was there that Paul proclaimed to the larger synagogue congregation that Jesus, because of his resurrection from the dead, was obviously the long-awaited Messiah. There were twelve of those who heard Paul who responded and were baptized, and were empowered by the Holy Spirit to speak in tongues, to witness miracles and healings, and who obviously became quite contagious in their faith. Paul evidently met with his smaller group in a disciple-making fellowship for many months. Paul also taught publicly in the synagogue for three months, or until he was asked to leave by resistant synagogue leaders. He then moved to a rented hall and taught them for two years. You see, then, the recurring pattern of larger assemblies for public teaching and smaller groups for more intense disciple making.

Whatever the dynamics, it was fruitful in the missionary calling of the church, because the Acts account of this Ephesus episode says that through this expression of an intentional community of discipleship "all the residents of Asia [Minor] heard the word of the Lord" (Acts 19:10).

There is, then, a very significant place for public teaching in larger assemblies, but the working heart of the church is those colonies where everyone has a name and a face, and a story, and where it is small enough so that all are both accountable to one another and responsible for one another. In my own long career as a pastor and teacher in the church, this twofold pattern has guided me. I have sought to carefully teach the Scriptures to the larger church community, but I have also sought to discern those who responded to spend time with me (and often a smaller group of others) in the disciple-making disciplines, and in learning the disciplines of mutual accountability and responsibility. I hasten to say that such persons and groups have not been shy in holding me accountable also, which is a great gift to me. Such beautiful relationships continue between many of us, though circumstances have separated us geographically for many years.

Another helpful image comes to me from a friend of mine who was an avid mountain climber earlier in his life. He has given me a graphic metaphor of those two forms of Christian community. He designates the larger assemblies as those *staging areas* for aspiring mountain climbers (often novices at such a challenge) in which potential mountaineers are taught by the veterans about the disciplines and dangers, the logistical requirements, and the physical conditioning necessary for safely ascending what are potentially hazardous mountains. But the working groups who actually climb the mountains form themselves into *base camps,* or those small groups who do the ascent together, and who are responsible for each other very knowledgeably. Those base camps are where the climbers encourage and instruct one another, knowing that their successful accomplishment of the summit is dependent on each other. My conclusion is that, as those who are Christ's disciples, those *aliens and exiles* who are engaged daily in all of the delights and hazards of this journey . . . we need both forms—staging areas and base camps—when at all possible.

Or maybe the humorous metaphor given us by Wes Seeliger in his *Western Theology* (sadly out of print) will be helpful to a degree. In his humorous caricature he offers two paradigms, or images, for the church—one is good and the other misses the point of it all. He uses the old West as his setting, and he describes two kinds of images of the church. The one that he derides is that of the *settlers*, who want the security and order of a small town, what with a sheriff and rules, and where the church is conceived of at the town meeting in the courthouse on Sunday, and where God is the mayor. The other image is that the church is like a wagon train seeking an unknown destination and experiencing all kinds of hazards. Seeliger's good image, then, is that of the church made up of *pioneers*. On the trail, all of the pioneers share the hazards of the journey, and the uncertain destination, but all are dependent on each other, and God is the trail boss, who shares all the hazards with his folk, and gets down into the mud to help them get their wagons unstuck. That's colorful theology, but makes the point of the form and lifestyle of a pilgrim community.

The One-Another Factor

Christ's calling of us does not necessitate large numbers. Jesus even noted that *"where two or three are gathered in my name, there am I among them"* (Matt 18:20). That comment says far more than it appears at first blush. It speaks of small units of his *New Humanity* that are somehow his dwelling place, and are therefore authentic elements in the church. When you pursue the *one-another* references throughout the New Testament, however, you get a wonderfully rich composite of the dynamics of the colonies of the *New Creation*. Just consider: love one another, forgive one another, bear one another's burdens, confess you sins to one another, live in harmony with one another, forbear with one another in love, teach and admonish one another in all wisdom . . . and so much more. What emerges here is a thrilling picture of a whole new kind of human community where Christ indwells each member, and where each member becomes Christ to the others by the Holy Spirit.

Such profound community can never be large or impersonal (such has often been true in large expressions of institutional Christianity). Such colonies formed by the Word of Christ and the Spirit of Christ have got to be the basic form of the church, and the form in which the formational disciplines are always in play, as each person ministers to the others, and where the more mature persons mentor the less mature persons, and where the strong take special concern for the weak. Even with those large church assemblies where public teaching is the focus, it is critical that there be those small colonies in which the *one-another* component is wrought out in real lives. That also may take many forms, and is continually reinventing itself to conform to different circumstances and challenges.

Such dynamics presupposes also the ongoing discipline of repentance—that the forsaking of our autonomy and self-focus is always in the process of being replaced by the servant-spirit of Jesus Christ. The fruits of the Holy Spirit always include humility, long-suffering, patience, gentleness, and those characteristics that were true of our Lord Jesus Christ. The fruits of the Holy Spirit are the fruits of Christ dwelling in and forming the character of those whom he calls. We are, consequently, accountable to each other in this transformational process.

". . . Not Neglecting to Meet Together . . ."

Just before we move on to the next consideration in answer to our question, "*What on earth is the church?*" . . . there is the word from the writer of the Letter to the Hebrews that Christ's people not neglect to meet together and spend time with one another. It is a negative factor in our formation into the image of Christ when we intentionally, or inadvertently, isolate ourselves from others. It is a critical discipline that we meet with others of our colony of pilgrims and strangers on a regular basis, if at all possible. Our calling is out of our privacy and into this new race of humanity that Christ is forming. Again, that can take place in any one of innumerable venues and forms. Sometimes circumstances of time and distance make this complicated. In our social media age, sometimes it is accomplished of necessity only by such means. Still, we must find some way in which we are never out of communication and fellowship with those with whom we are bound together in some *one-another* covenant.

Such may find their incarnation in scenes of cultural hostility and darkness, and be accomplished only with great skill and discreetness. At the same time, it is in the greatest darkness that such colonies of light and love shine most brightly as God's alternative narrative to the brokenness and longing of that lost humanity which Jesus came to seek and to save.

The form is not the primary focus, but the formation of the persons, in whatever form the colony takes, into the image of Christ—that is the focus. It begins with two or three, perhaps, but it is to be the fragrant aroma of Christ unto God. It is the colony of those who have come intentionally through Christ the Door, and in whom Christ dwells forming them into his image. The form will always be changing, and it will always be in process until that ultimate day when all is consummated, and the Bride of Christ is perfected. Before us is always that new heaven and new earth, and the declaration comes: "*Behold, the dwelling place of God is with man. He will dwell with them, and they will be his people, and God himself will be with them as their God. He will wipe away every tear from their eyes, and death shall be no more . . . for the former things have passed away*" (Rev 21:3–4). For us, meanwhile, the church is the dwelling place of God by the Spirit, and is in the process of being recreated, looking forward to that day.

— 7 —

MODELS AND MENTORS

Just maybe, however, there is a question behind the questions we have been pursuing. After all, to ask *"What on earth is the church?"* assumes that it is not some sterile, totally irrelevant, impersonal religious society oblivious to questions that haunt us—questions about meaning and acceptance and hope. Further, to designate the church as the community of God's *New Humanity* would require as one of its components the meaningful and nurturing relationships necessary for such. That then leads us to the next question: Who are the real persons who constitute such communities? Who are those who have been there before me, and can show me the way, and answer my questions, and demonstrate the reality of it all? Who are the real persons who authentically incarnate the four dimensions of our *algorithm* described above? Who are the practitioners of *New Creation*, the models? Who are those who can mentor the inquirer into such new life? We do not experience such communities in a vacuum.

We're not looking here for those impressive large religious institutions that exist under the rubric of being "the church." They are there, of course, and some of them are remarkable forums for good teaching, while many others are moribund and archaic relics of a former era. But that's a whole other subject, and not our focus here.

We're looking for those living colonies of God's *New Humanity* composed of those who have intentionally forsaken the broad way, have renounced their autonomous ways, and have come to Jesus Christ . . . those who have responded to his call and who have entered the whole new (and often bewildering) life created in them by the Holy Spirit—they are in process of being recreated into the image of God. We're looking for those who are the incarnation of the new race being called by Jesus Christ, those in process of becoming the truly human men and women whom God is creating by his own Spirit. The colonies we're looking for are made up of such, and are those who have bound themselves to one another, and in which colonies all have names and faces and stories known to one another. Such colonies are made up of real persons, real others who are, just as you and me, sinners in that process of being made new. Their numbers may be as small as two or three . . . but someone in that configuration will emerge as the one to whom the others look for encouragement, and to assist them in forming this totally new kind of community, and orienting them into it.

Life in God's *New Humanity* is, after all, God's own life inhabiting such as we by his Spirit. If the New Testament scriptures are to be our authority and our guiding line, then we find in them some staggering instructions, such as this, for instance: "*Therefore be imitators of God, as beloved children. And walk in love, as Christ loved us and gave himself up for us, a fragrant offering and sacrifice to God*" (Eph 5:1). Imitators of God? What does that look like? Who are the formative figures within the colony or community who mentor others in the knowledge, the wisdom, and into the maturity and fruitfulness that makes the whole church something of the fragrance of Christ in the midst of the larger human community. Who shows us how to live into that radically "other" *New Humanity*? Who keeps the community on track, i.e., who keeps it true to its calling by Christ?

For starters, then, let's look at those in any given colony of Christ's followers who are the disciple makers, those who walk alongside others and mentor them into the image of God. Such disciple making was beautifully modeled by Jesus himself when he called the Twelve to come walk along with him and live close to him for those many months. One does not remain a stranger when he or she allows others to get close and spend significant time with one.

The answers to our questions here find all kinds of answers in the New Testament accounts of Jesus' own dealing with the Twelve that are practical jewels. His example and modeling pertains to any colony of his *New Creation* and for the actual life of vital communities of the kingdom of God. It is a whole different and refreshing kind of leadership modeled and taught by Christ himself. For instance, when his own disciples were jockeying for positions of prominence, he gave them an answer that was also a rebuke to any power hungry leadership: *"whoever would be great among you must be your servant, and whoever would be first among you must be your slave"* (Matt 20:26–27). That selfsame principle is put forward by the apostle later in a letter to a church: *"Have this mind among yourselves, which is yours in Christ Jesus, who, though he was in the form of God, did not count equality with God a thing to be grasped, but emptied himself, by taking the form of a servant"* (Phil 2:5–7).

The answer to our questions about leadership in such colonies is that leadership emerges in the more mature persons, who in their new life in Christ become the models and mentors for the rest. It was Paul who was quite candid in his word to the church in Philippi: *"What you have learned and received and heard and seen in me—practice these things, and the God of peace will be with you"* (Phil 4:9). Or, *"Be imitators of me, as I am of Christ"* (1 Cor 11:1).

Those of this present emerging generation in which we live are drowning in advertising, what with all of the claims and counterclaims of the consumer culture that dominate so much of the media. What is persuasive to us, however, is when something is obviously so compelling that it cannot be dismissed. The church is intended to be just such an authentic non-dismissible demonstration of such true community, of such reconciling relationships, and of such demonstrations of the message of Christ (as spelled out in the four dimensions of our *algorithm* above) that are inescapably persuasive when we encounter them. Such are the flesh-and-blood evidences of those who have found meaning and hope and love in Christ, and are living that new life out compellingly and (how to say it?) in *transformational relationships* with one another, i.e., relationships that are dynamically obvious within that community.

That should not sound strange, considering where we have been in this guide. It is God's design in Christ to make all things new. It is recorded that those who are called to his purpose . . . are also predestined to be *conformed to the image of his Son*, which brings us back to the question: Who models such? Who shows us the way and mentors us into such a radical new kind of life? What are the dynamics?

So, yes, the Spirit does in fact come to indwell us when we enter Christ the Door, but such doesn't usually happen apart from colonies of God's *New Humanity* (in whatever form), and apart from those others who have become Christ to one another—the recreated human community in Christ. Then, back to our quest: What should we look for in those who (perhaps modestly, and with hesitation to assume such responsibility) become the leaders, or the formative persons, in such colonies? So here let me reiterate that it begins with a person's being willing to be transparent, and to allow others to get close, to spend significant time with others until they are able to mentor those others into a degree of maturity, or until they are reproductive of the image of Christ themselves. It's called *disciple making*. Jesus spent two years teaching, modeling, and mentoring his disciples, until he had basically reproduced himself in them—which only became clear to them after his resurrection and the descent of the Holy Spirit.

There Is No Such Category as Clergy in the New Testament Church

Let's stop right here, and let me say that we're not talking about any special or *sacralized* class of men or women who are called "clergy." When the question of *clergy* is raised with me, my response is: yes and no. We have lived with that designation in the previous patterns of the church. There are so many incredibly marvelous servants of God who have blessed and formed others, and who were so designated. (Alas! there are also many charlatans, empire builders, needy egos, charismatic personalities, and other questionable sorts who love to be called "Reverend" or "Doctor." I don't want to go there.) I myself am the recipient of the equipping gifts of many of gifted and godly folk who were designated as clergy. That being said, there is no such category to be found anywhere in the New Testament documents. If anything, every single one of the people of God is called into the *ministry* of the *New Creation* by virtue of his or her baptism. All of God's people are called to be priests unto God (Rev 1:6), and are to be formed for that ministry within the colonies of God's New Creation. The church is a nation of priests (1 Pet 2:9). There is never anywhere an instruction to call anyone "Reverend." What *is* taught is that *all* are to be formed more and more into the image and mind of Christ, and *all* are to be the incarnation of Christ, and to be servants to each other, and *all* of that in the midst of whatever context they inhabit.

Paul gives us one clue when he tells young Timothy to "*entrust* [the gospel] *to faithful men who will be able to teach others also*" (2 Tim 2:2). Peter addresses the elders of the church about the seriousness of their calling to be leaders by identifying himself also as a fellow elder (something like a mature wisdom figure recognized as such by the community), and telling them that their being the shepherds to God's flock and having oversight of God's people requires that they also be, especially, examples or models, who are ultimately responsible to the chief Shepherd, to Jesus for, those for whom they are responsible in the community. They are always to clothe themselves in humility toward one another because God opposes those who are proud and gives grace to the humble (1 Pet 5:1–5).

Elsewhere in the writings of Paul, regarding the qualifications of those who have been acknowledged as the leaders, he makes a strong point about the necessity of such integrity and authenticity in their new lives in Christ—that it is acknowledged not only by those inside the community, but even by those outside of the community of faith. Leaders are to be the authentic, mature, and knowledgeable practitioners of God's *New Creation*. They are to be formed by the Word of Christ and able to teach it. Peter reminds the church that it is by our knowledge of, and faithfulness to, the message of Christ that the divine nature is formed in us. The primary bonding element is the love of God working in and through them.

Somewhere along the line, however, there entered the church's tradition the questionable notion that leadership could be bestowed by achieving an academic degree in theology, or some such credentials achieved in institutions other than the colonies in and to which one is called. Such is an aberration, if not a downright subversion, of the God-given plan. The use of the mind in the service of God is inarguably, of course, part of our worship. Every believer should make skill in Scripture a lifelong quest, even those in oral cultures where Scripture must be memorized. But it is the *praxis* of Christ's calling that makes *New Humanity* visible to the world, and is the necessity for leadership within the church.

We also need to stop right here and be reminded that if there is no such model and mentor apparent, then it might fall to you to get with your Bible as a guide, and to give yourself to prayer, and ask God to form you into just such a person.

"Wait a Minute, Bob, You're Clergy. What Gives?"

Ah yes, a word of self-disclosure is in order here. I began my career in the standard and unquestioned pattern of my church at that time in my youth, when one became a *minister of the gospel* by deciding that such would be a good career. Then the procedure was to come under the oversight of a governing body and attend a theological school. That was followed by receiving a rite called "ordination." All that accomplished, one was ostensibly qualified to be a church leader, or pastor, and then put out on the market to become the pastor of some church. That was my pattern. That was what was expected. But I was actually more practically formed by my engagement with my own father, who was such a model to our local congregation. After that, as a young adult, I was taken seriously and mentored into a clearer understanding of the Christian life in a summer Bible conference. The folk who led that summer community *discipled* me, and were much more formative in equipping me than anything I experienced in my formal theological education.

Also, I was hugely formed "in the trenches" through my role as campus pastor to university students, who were relentless in asking difficult questions, and totally unintimidated by my ecclesiastical status. In addition to that was my long-distance formation through my association with the resources of Inter-Varsity Christian Fellowship, which put the focus on discipleship, on the disciplines of Christian living, and on the mission of reaching others for Christ.

That all being so, then I redefined for my own self-understanding what my role was to be in church leadership. That understanding was that I was to have, in fact, a public role as a skillful teacher of the Word of God through the exposition of the Scriptures in public gatherings for worship. But, more primarily, I would have the role of being a model and a mentor for those responsive men and women who attached themselves to me in a *one-another* relationship, which relationship to me, and my attachment to them, made them my spiritual children in the Lord.

In more recent years, in my post-retirement role as something of an encourager through a ministry to students and faculty in a number of theological institutions, I have found that there is very little focus on such modeling and mentoring in their curricula, except occasionally where it emerged as an essential component in the discipline of missiology, i.e., the study of the mission of God. Also, to my observation, it was not within the self-understanding of many of the faculty of those institutions that they themselves had any role as the ostensible equippers, mentors, and models to their students. I find myself, therefore (as missiologist David Bosch described those of us so formed), a *gadfly* in the traditional church. So, now I hope I have confessed to you what may appear a self-contradiction, and what it is that motivates such a writing as this one . . . or I may have totally confused you.

New Creation Colonies Are to Have Order and Oversight, Along with Mentors

So yes, when we're asking *"What on earth is the church?"* we are not looking for any such thing as communities of merely chaotic spiritual enthusiasm. From the calling of Israel those millennia ago, God has always provided *structure* and order for his people, beginning with fairly small units. So also, the initial church in Jerusalem had resident within it those who had been Christ's disciples, who were acknowledged as the ones to teach and form that emerging missional community in the teachings of Christ, and it was they who were to assist in making the practical decisions that were inevitable in all of the newness as that church grew exponentially, and as multitudes were being added daily.

Very soon, however, the church began to move out into the larger world beyond Jerusalem, as the followers of Christ were contagious to share the thrilling news of Christ in their travels. The gospel was, to say it, out of control. At the same time, there do seem emerge a couple of factors in the New Testament regarding the need of leadership and order.

One factor was this: In each emerging colony of the *New Creation* there emerged quite naturally those who obviously got the message and were more mature and wise and knowledgeable about the teachings of Jesus, even though they might be quite young in the faith (though there is a warning about not making a new convert a leader in the church, lest they be lifted up with pride and become a problem [1 Tim 3:6]). We find, then, several designations of leadership. One is that there were *bishops*, which Greek word simply conveys the idea of oversight—sort of acknowledged leaders of the colony, who were responsible for keeping watch over the souls of God's people, and to whose leadership the community was to be properly submissive. That continues quite naturally in the present in emerging new church plants, and in house churches, or colonies, in many innovative forms and places.

It appears that a similar, if not synonymous, role is that of *elder* (or *presbyter*), which Greek word conveys exactly that, i.e., those who are perhaps a bit older and wiser in the faith, and more mature, and who have the same calling to give leadership by way of example and maturity, and so are to be the models and mentors for the rest. Such wisdom figures, who were mature in knowledge and behavior, emerged from within the community. It was also true that when such were proven and fruitful, they could in fact be sent, or encouraged to become part of the mission to plant and establish other churches, as the church grew and moved out into the larger world.

There also emerged within those early communities those gifted persons described as *deacons*. Their qualifications were very similar to those of the elders or bishops, except that their particular focus seems to have been the meeting of human need, and the care of those who were helpless—both those inside the community and also those among whom the church lived. That gift is, by the way, something of an interesting illustration of the *lifestyle* dimension of our four-fold *algorithm* that we visited earlier.

The other significant factor we discover in the New Testament that is so very critical for our consideration here, and so often ignored or overlooked... is that the risen Lord gives *gifts* (or *charismata*) to the church for the equipping of his people for their participation in its mission in and to the world. What the risen Lord knows is: that such healthy colonies of *New Humanity* require that every follower of Jesus be equipped to *maturity*, and so be a functioning part of the Body of Christ—no passivity when Christ is being formed in them. To that end there are listed four such equipping gifts (Eph 4:1–16). That text doesn't articulate exactly how or in whom such gifts are expressed, but the clear implication is that every believer is to be equipped in all four dimensions of the mission of God in the world. It would appear that no one is exempt from the need to be so equipped.

Models and Mentors

The needed dimensions are that all of God's people need to be equipped in the knowledge and praxis of the Word of Christ, and to that end the gift of *pastor-teacher* is given. Each believer is to be equipped to know how to fruitfully engage in communicating the message to those outside—in conversation, or however—and so there is the gift of *evangelist*. Then all of God's people need to know how to interpret or exegete the precise cultural setting in which they live daily, and also of the larger world and culture, and so there is the gift of *prophet*. And finally, to the surprise of most, every believer is to be equipped to be a missionary church planter, however that comes about in his or her career, and so there is the gift of *apostle*. Somehow, every believer is to have the role of looking for occasions to be part of God's mission in his or her home, or neighborhood, or workplace—to be living out Christ's calling to be the church.

Yes, such are the equipping gifts, but there are other lists of (what I call) *household gifts*, given as the church had some specific need of skills or ministries, and so such gifts emerged when special needs required them. There were also some miraculous gifts, such as healing and worshipping in tongues. The several lists of such gifts are all different, and give us a flavor of particular needs that emerged along the way, and for which God provided gifted persons.

Here again, there is no place for passive non-participation within the colonies of God's *New Humanity*. Yet here again, it is essential that those being so equipped need models and mentors, i.e., those to show them how to engage it all. One isn't equipped in those four gifts by sitting in a classroom. One learns them by spending time with someone who is authentic and wholesomely engaged in practicing them. Learning has its positive and negative components. In the church's mission to the world there is always spiritual conflict as the light clashes with the darkness. Then there are inevitably all of the diverse and sometimes pathological, or totally screwed up, personalities who appear in the colony. One learns how to engage such only by watching someone who is mature and wise confronting such. There would obviously be a profound overlap between those four equipping gifts and the role of the elders-bishops. Those who are the models of Christ to the community are to those who, as such, are free and transparent, and so able and willing to allow others to get close and observe then engaging the difficulties of communal life. The goal is that the models and mentors themselves are to be models of new life in Christ.

When such order is being incarnated, and where all of God's people are being equipped in such gifts, then it becomes a reality that the believers in our colonies of God's *New Humanity* are able, indeed, to "teach and admonish each other with psalms and hymns and spiritual songs," and where the Word of Christ "dwells richly" among them, as described in the Letter to the Colossians (3:16). Such colonies don't just happen. They require formation. Such formation requires the presence of those who are able to expedite that formation, to model it, and to mentor others into mature participation.

Such Modeling and Mentoring Is Only Possible in Smaller Configurations

Before we go on, it may be worth a bit of defining here. This need for models and mentors is precisely what Christ's commission for us to *make disciples* is all about. It is inescapably focused on individual and real persons. Disciple making and the role of models and mentors are essentially the same reality, and speak to the very same necessity within the colonies of God's *New Humanity*. The practical reality, however, is (take note) that such is not possible in any larger group when a person can be anonymous or unaccountable. Modeling and mentoring, of necessity, require a very dynamic, person-oriented, and mutual focus on the *one-another* relationship between the mentor and the person being mentored (or discipled). It is basically within such a relationship that those who are new to Christ's calling come to understand how such a life is wrought out in one's thinking and behavior, and in the practical, or existential, realities of everyday life. It can only be partially and

Models and Mentors

inadequately accomplished in large groups. The reality is, however, that many who have come through the Door have also inadvertently found themselves in some kind of a "do it yourself" situation where they could only seek to form themselves to the teachings of Christ. To such the Spirit of God is ever faithful in so enabling them. But the design of God is still that each colony have that one, or those several, who model the faith and encourage the others into its reality in their ordinary lives.

Every believer in Christ is to be a disciple maker, and from his or her entry into Christ is to be such a person in training. As one is formed into the image of Christ, then that one has Christ's *disciple-making DNA* in his or her life. That is the formation of the "*missionary arm of the Holy Trinity*" dimension of our fourfold *algorithm*, by which the Christian colony is evident to the world. It is a vital part of having Christ in us. Lives and colonies so formed can be observed by the quietly authentic inner reality of the divine nature in their ordinary lives.

The mentors and models are also those who demonstrate what such practitioners of the fourfold equipping gifts of the Holy Spirit look like in flesh and blood. They are those who approximate the goal of those equipping gifts we looked at previously. If all of this sounds too idealistic, it is also true to acknowledge here that, in reality, it is often those who are the most mature and the most beautiful in their demonstration of their mature lives in Christ who are also the most self-effacing, and in their true humility resist being called into leadership positions, even when they are acknowledged models for others.

Conversely, it is those who *need* to be leaders, or elders, and who push themselves before the rest—who *need* authority, who have ego needs—who should be avoided since they are devoid of the humility and the servant heart that is called for in demonstrating Christ's life to the community.

To conclude this particular chapter, God knows that his children need spiritual parents, those who can show them the way and demonstrate the life of Christ in the communities of his

New Humanity. It is always wonderful when there are those who are, somehow, in their real humanity, a "sweet aroma of Christ." It is always so encouraging to find those who are contagious with the message of God's love in Christ—of his grace and truth. It is also enormously helpful to have those who are practitioners of the lifestyle of God's *New Creation*, especially under often-stressful circumstances and difficult contexts. It is so very heartening, likewise, to have among us those who model loving, reconciling relationships.

Any follower of Christ can aspire to be a leader and a wholesome model to others, and all should so aspire, but such persons can only confirm their authenticity as they model the radical new life that is ours in Christ—his image incarnated in persons such as us.

— 8 —

THE MYSTERY BEHIND THE MYSTERY

There really is no way we can pursue our quest to know what on earth the church is all about without coming ultimately to this juncture, where we must admit that the whole reality defies any category of human rationality within which our modern culture operates.

There is a mystery behind the mystery of the church. There is a drama behind the drama of the church. There is a cosmic conflict involved in our understanding of the church. The church, in its integrity, is not humanly explainable. It should not even exist. After all, it had very remote and modest beginnings, and from its very inception incurred the hostility of both the religious establishment of Jerusalem and the Roman Empire—and yet it not only survived but became a hugely influential factor in those first centuries of its existence. What's going on?

Perhaps we need to begin by rehearsing the episode at Caesarea Philippi that we looked at in an earlier chapter, and unpack it a bit more. After spending many months with his small band of his disciples, Jesus asked them on that particular day, "Who do people say that I am?" They reported the various responses they had heard. Then he asked them, "But who do you say that I am?" To that question Peter gave their answer: "You are the Christ, the

Son of the living God" (Matt 16:15–16). Now, let's slow down here and listen carefully to how Jesus responds to that, because it opens the window to realities that are far more profound than anything merely religious. First of all, it is my judgment that Jesus engages in a pun, since the name *Peter* means "rock" (Greek: *petros*). Jesus says, in essence, "Yes, you are Peter, but it is upon this rock, i.e., your testimony that I am the Messiah, that I am going to build my *church*, and (take note) *the gates of hell shall not prevail against it.*"

There are two realities here that are essential to our quest. First of all, Jesus appropriates the common Greek word *ekklesia* (meaning "*called out*"), which can refer to any group that might be *called out* for some specific purpose, whether to advocate a cause, or celebrate some occasion, or engage in political activity—it is not a religious or Christian word at all. It was only in giving it translation into English many centuries later that the translators chose the word *church* (using a word that signifies it in early English as a community belonging to the Lord) as its English counterpart. The point we need to come to grips with, however, is this: If this *ekklesia* that Jesus is going to create, or build, as a people "called out," then we need to ask immediately: "Called *out of* what?" And then, "Called *into* what?" (And ultimately *for* what?) That, in turn, implies that there are a couple of competing but unseen human communities out there that we need to explore. One of them has to do with the disciples' affirmation that Jesus was Messiah, and the other is some kind of expression of whatever "the gates of hell" is all about.

So let's ramble about in the biblical narrative for a bit, because these two realities are there from the outset. The word *Messiah* in the Jewish culture referred to God's "Anointed One," and was an expectation within that culture for centuries. It all begins with the creation story, right at the outset of human history. Look at the account, first of all, of the intrusion of a negative, supernatural, accusing, destructive figure—a serpent *"more crafty than any other beast of the field that God had made"*—who incited an act of disobedience into that harmonious scene by suggesting to those first persons that they could be their own gods, and thereby not be

The Mystery Behind the Mystery

captive or subservient to the supposedly restrictive commands of their Creator. What God had forbidden, mind you, was for their own good. What with all of the figurative images of that primordial account, God's loving intention was that those first parents should never have to experience the reality and consequences of evil,[1] which tragic experience would happen through their partaking of the fruit of the tree that was called "the tree of the knowledge of good and evil" (Gen 2:17).

But immediately after those first humans succumbed to the serpent's (Satan's) rebellion, God told them of the pain it would bring . . . God also made a promise that somehow in his good purpose for his creation there would come the seed of a woman who would ultimately and mortally wound the serpent's head (Gen 3:15). That is our first clue of what would emerge in the following generations as the idea of a *Messiah*, an Anointed One—a redemptive figure to deal with the serpent, to deal with the guilt of the rebellious creation, and to ultimately restore God's *Shalom* by making all things new. (I know I'm jumping the gun here, but I want my readers to know what is before them in what follows). So we have two realities introduced: *condemnation* and *promise*. Enter two other realities: God's design for his creation and his ultimate dominion, and also a rebellious dominion somehow energized by a malignant and supernatural personality. Our human scene and history do not exist in neutral territory.

To repeat: Two things, then, come from this primordial bit of folk history (passed down for generations in an oral culture) in the third chapter of Genesis. First was the condemnation of the serpent, Satan, and the *promise* that it would be "the seed of a woman" who would ultimately bring about his end. Second, however, was a *defiled creation* in which humankind would experience what they had sought: namely, a life in which they would bear the results of their attempted autonomy and estrangement from God, as they sought to be their own gods. God's response to their act of rebellion

---

1. *Evil* might be described (or maybe oversimplified) as life without God, or moral boundaries, or meaning, or absolutes/authority. As such it can even be *religious* or *spiritual*.

was to describe their now tragic present reality . . . and then to give them a future hope. The present reality is a defiled human community, and also one who is an adversary of God—Satan. It was, in that first hint about the seed of a woman, however, that the concept of an *Anointed One* begins to emerge, though ever so dimly. And it is in the demonstration of the presence of an accusing adversary of God that there first comes to our attention something of "the gates of hell" entity. Present reality and future promise. God has a plan and will not ultimately be thwarted.

Again, in some of the earliest documents of the recorded history, we have in our biblical narrative an episode that took place millennia before Jesus. It took place out there in the Middle East, and in which episode God revealed himself through angelic messengers to a godly sheik by the name of Abram (or Abraham), and revealed to him that in his seed (singular) all the nations of the earth should be blessed. Strange occurrence! That encounter is the genesis of the Jewish nation and culture and hope. It is the beginning of the Hebrew nation, whose history is what we have before us in those documents that we now call the "Old Testament." That promise to Abraham kept emerging as the centuries rolled by, and all that time there was gestating in the corporate psyche of the Jewish people the sense that somehow they were special among the nations. But then . . . they would periodically forget that, and so revert to some conformity to the nations around them. But in this biblical ramble of ours, there emerges, with the reign of David as king of the Jewish people (1010–970 BCE), another reminder of the promise. His reign was the high-water mark of Jewish history. The reminder of the promise was that somehow it would be the seed of David that would be the Anointed of God, or the *Messiah*. It would be his seed that would bring about a forever kingdom, a *New Creation*.

Then, in eighth and seventh centuries before Christ, in a period in which the Jewish nation had fallen into much decay, and had even been taken into captivity, there emerged a group of unique (and often eccentric) prophets, who began to fill in some of the details of what that anticipated *Anointed of God*, that *Messiah*,

The Mystery Behind the Mystery

would accomplish. Those details included not only the making of all things new, not only the creation of the peaceable kingdom of *Shalom* . . . but also that the *Messiah* would deal with the tragic results and guilt of the human rebellion. He would bear their guilt and become the sin offering for them in order to reconcile them to God. He would heal them, and bring about a *New Creation* in which the very divine nature of God, the mind of God and the will of God, would be displayed in his people. All of that, however, would be accomplished at an enormous price borne by God himself in love.

That expectation and that hope were very much alive in the consciousness of a remnant of godly Jews. It was prayed for, and hoped for, by them. And it is with that expectation of the visit of God in a *Messiah* that we enter the New Testament narrative. Again, an angelic messenger came to a young virgin (one of the godly remnant) by the name of Mary. The angel told her that she was to be the chosen vessel to give birth to the long-awaited *Messiah*, the one who would sit on the throne of David, and of whose kingdom there would be no end. (The miraculous events of the nativity of Jesus and of its cosmic and eschatological significance tend to be obscured by present-day Christmas commercial orgies, but let's not go there.)

You may be asking by now, "What is Satan up to all this time?" Yes, the plot thickens. Note that after the birth of Jesus there was an attempt to murder him by the half-breed Jewish king Herod. God warned Jesus' parents of the plot and they took refuge in Egypt. After Herod's death the family returned to the small city of Nazareth. From that point there is little history of their family life, other than the record of their brief visit to the temple when Jesus was twelve years old. It is worth noting, however, that on that visit the priests in the temple were awed at Jesus' questions and at his knowledge of the Scriptures.

It is only when Jesus was about thirty years old that his cousin John (also born under unusual circumstances), who himself was something of an eccentric prophet, attracted much attention by his preaching to Jewish people that they should repent because the

Messiah was coming soon. John preached out in the wilderness, and was baptizing those penitent Jews who responded in the Jordan River. It was onto this scene that Jesus quietly made his first public appearance, and there he requested of his cousin John that he be baptized (perhaps to show his solidarity with the other godly Israelites). John knew something of Jesus' own miraculous birth, about the promises made to his mother, and because of that he initially objected to baptizing Jesus. His response to Jesus was that he, John, should actually be baptized *by* Jesus. But Jesus prevailed and so was baptized. John reported that, as he was baptizing Jesus, he saw the Holy Spirit descending on Jesus in the form of a dove, and heard a voice from heaven saying, "*This is my beloved Son, with whom I am well pleased*" (Matt 3:17).

In the drama behind the drama of the church, or in answer to our overarching question, "*What on earth is the church?*" . . . what happened next is very revealing. Jesus left his baptismal scene, and then, as the narrative states, the Spirit led him into the wilderness, and for forty days he was there being tempted—and guess by *whom?* . . . Yes, you guessed it, by Satan, the devil, the prince of darkness! It seems obvious that the devil somehow understood exactly who Jesus was, and somehow had the foreboding that Jesus had come as God's Anointed One to challenge his own satanic dominion of darkness. At the same time, there was a critical blank spot in Satan's knowledge as to exactly how Jesus was going to accomplish that which he had been sent to do by his Father in heaven. True to his subversive and malicious nature, however, Satan offered Jesus all kinds of enticing temptations as alternative ways to become great and powerful and popular, i.e., to become a Messiah-figure . . . but they all depended on Jesus succumbing to Satan's proposals. To each temptation, Jesus responded with his absolute fidelity to that which his Father had commissioned him to be and do as the dearly beloved Son.[2]

In our ramble through Scripture, skip over (for the moment) to the events of Jesus' earthly ministry, of his time spent with his

---

2. The apostle Paul would refer to Jesus as the second Adam, who became a life-giving spirit (1 Cor 15:45).

The Mystery Behind the Mystery

disciples, of his arrest, crucifixion, resurrection, and ascension. Skip over to late in the first century, when the newness and all of the rearranging of the disciples' understanding had taken place. The dust had settled, and the apostles and the church had time to reflect on the meaning of it all, and on their mission. It is in one of the later New Testament documents that the apostle John, who was as close to Jesus as any (and was also very close to Jesus' mother, who was a primary eyewitness to it all), wrote a general letter to some unnamed churches. Among other things, he states such an awesome understanding of the meaning of Jesus' life and ministry as: "*The reason the Son of God appeared was to destroy the works of the devil*"; and "*We know that we are from God, and the whole world lies in the power of the evil one*" (1 John 3:8b; 5:19). Or perhaps it will help us to remember the commission of the risen Lord to Paul: "*I am sending you to them to open their eyes and turn them from darkness to light, and from the power of Satan to God, so that they may receive forgiveness of sins and a place among those who are sanctified by faith in me*" (Acts 26:17–18, NIV). Or, perhaps this word of illumination from Paul's letter to the Christians at Colossae: "*He* [Jesus] *has delivered us from the domain of darkness and transferred us to the kingdom of his beloved Son, in whom we have redemption, the forgiveness of sins*" (Col 1:13–14).

That clash of kingdoms is precisely what Jesus knew when he entered his public ministry, when he encountered the temptations by Satan in the wilderness. He was profoundly aware of, and formed by, his Father's love for the world. He knew of, and was obedient to, the Father's will to bring true redemption from all of the blight of the darkness Satan had provoked. Jesus also knew all of the symptoms of that darkness, and its tragic results.

So it was after his wilderness testing, and when he returned to his home synagogue in Nazareth on the Sabbath, that he was given the privilege of reading the lesson for the day. The assigned passage for that day was the messianic prophecy from Isaiah 61 about the Lord's favor that would be visited when God's *New Creation* would be inaugurated by the *Messiah*. That text speaks of the anointing of the Spirit upon God's anointed servant, who would bring good news to the poor, ministry to the brokenhearted, liberty to the captives, the opening of prison to those who are bound, and the proclamation of the year of the Lord's favor (Luke 4:18–19). All of that speaks of the ministry of the Lord's anointed, the *Messiah*.

Jesus then handed the scroll back to the attendant, and then said, "Today this Scripture has been fulfilled in your hearing" (Luke 4:21). The folk in the synagogue went ballistic, and berated him. They knew him. He was a local boy. To them it was blasphemous that Jesus make such claims. Their response reminds us that the dominion of darkness was very much in place even in Jesus' home synagogue.

After he escaped their rage, he began his public ministry, actually demonstrating the very evidences of God's *New Creation* that he had read to the synagogue from Isaiah about the mission of the *Messiah*. He taught about the *New Creation* (the kingdom of God). He demonstrated it. He healed the sick, and fed the hungry, and even raised the dead. Some of those individuals who were early responders to his teachings would become his intimate disciples, and he spent many months teaching and mentoring them about the unimaginable that was taking place in and through himself.

At one point, after John the Baptist had been imprisoned and was himself having some doubts about whether Jesus really was the promised Messiah, or whether they should look for another . . . John sent his disciples to Jesus with those doubts and that question. Jesus' response was that they should respond to John that all of the messianic signs prophesied by the earlier prophets were being fulfilled: "*Go and tell John what you have seen and heard: the blind receive their sight, the lame walk, lepers are cleansed, and the deaf hear, the dead are raised up, the poor have good news preached to them*" (Luke 7:22).

That Jesus was aware of the power of the dominion of darkness was evidenced in several occasions along the way. At one point, when he had send his disciples out on something like an interning mission to do what he had done and to teach what he had taught, they returned with glowing reports that "*even demons are subject to us.*" To this report Jesus responded, "*I saw Satan fall* like lightning from heaven. Behold, I have given you authority to tread on serpents and scorpions, and over all the power of the enemy" (Luke 10:17–19). And there was that particular moment, as he was telling his disciples about the necessity of his impending arrest and death, that Peter objected that such should happen, and Jesus' enigmatic response was, "*Get behind me, Satan! You are a hindrance to me*" (Matt 16:23).

Christ's calling to literally storm the gates of hell was always a very essential component in his sense of his messianic mandate. Even when he was being accused of all kinds of things at his arrest and arraignment, he questioned why they had chosen that moment to accuse him, but then he answered his own question: "*But this is your hour, and the power of darkness*" (Luke 22:53).

I have walked us through all of this simply to say that Jesus' word at Caesarea Philippi should be an unmistakable reality check for us, namely, that there are two very real dominions: there is that *dominion of the Messiah* into which he was calling a whole *New Humanity*, a reconciled community, or the people of the age to come; and then there is that other *dominion of darkness*, or *of Satan* and of condemnation, out of which he was calling his *New Creation* people. Such, of course, will never "sell" to the cynical modern mind, yet it is a very essential lens through which we need to look if we are to know what on earth the church is all about. The apostolic writings are much more specific, and we shall get to them presently.

There is a drama behind the drama of the church. There is a mystery behind the mystery of the church. One can never really understand what on earth the church *is* . . . unless one understands that it is a community with a very unmistakable sense that it has been called out of one dominion and into another—which is why *repentance and faith* are always at the entrance of God's *New Humanity*.

It is also a bit amusing that, with all of the inability of so much of the modern mind to accept such a view of reality as is portrayed in this biblical pattern, there should be such vastly popular fictional writings as the Harry Potter stories, or the Chronicles of

Narnia, or the Lord of the Rings trilogy, which become best-sellers on the basis of such conflicts between darkness and light. Most humans know that there is just such a cosmic mystery and drama, but find it difficult to embrace rationally. Human autonomy finds it difficult to cope with the concept of *evil*. The church, however, is built on the solid reality that, in and through Jesus, God is *calling out* an irresistible new community by his Spirit, and by his Spirit creating it again into its total harmony with the divine community.

But Back on Earth, How Does This All Play Out?

When a person discerns that Jesus Christ is the one in whom he or she finds hope and meaning and acceptance . . . in whom one finds a center, an authority, a creative source, and a guiding line, as well as a final goal . . . and enters through that Door into the new life of a child of God, then there is a transaction that takes place—yes, a supernatural transaction—in which, at the same time as one embraces Jesus Christ into his or her life, Christ simultaneously also indwells that person with his own life by the Spirit. That means that the divine DNA now becomes a dynamic force in the believer's life. It means that Christ, who is the Light, takes up residence in their very human lives and so initiates in them that dynamic process by which they are created as the sons and daughters of light.

At the same time, we need to stop here for a moment of truth. Such a transaction takes place in very real human beings, who have been called out of the dominion of darkness and into the dominion of God's dear Son. They come in all kinds of conditions. Some are really fractured and broken in many obvious ways. Some come out of intellectual darkness, or moral and ethical darkness. Some come totally confused and screwed up in many ways. Some come also with many commendable gifts and accomplishments, but all come with some sense of need or . . . with a vast emptiness that has driven them to seek meaning and hope. Some come alienated and oppressed, or discriminated against and persecuted. You name it, the church is composed of a huge mosaic of such real persons who now become part of God's *New Humanity*. Because this is so, sometimes the light that is to be present in such individuals and in the church shines rather dimly, but it is still there. It is always in process, and imperfect, but unmistakably there.

The church as the community of God's kingdom, God's *New Creation*, is to visibly demonstrate that light. Earlier, we named four visible dimensions, or demonstrations, so we will not revisit that here. But such communities are composed of individual persons who need the mutual encouragement, love, nurture, and accountability of others. That need requires a social unit small enough for each person to be known to one another with some intimacy, and this is never possible in large assemblies. The Silicon Valley wizards have concluded that the most effective creative groups are made up of about six persons all committed to the same compelling vision. That dynamic interaction among persons with the same common vision should also true of the communities of the light. Who, then, are the real persons to whom I am accountable? Who know my name? Who know my story? With whom I share this new life in Christ, and who have the same compelling vision as I?

Then comes the inevitable question: What are the disciplines of nurturing the light in *one another* that we need in order to employ to make all of that a reality? The *New Creation* that makes us to be lights in the darkness involves the renewal of our wills, of our minds, of our behavior, of our goals, and of our formative disciplines. Our new life by the Spirit provokes such disciplines. So what might they be?

Jesus spelled out the countercultural disciplines in his Sermon on the Mount (Matthew 5–7), or Sermon on the Plain (Luke 6), and told us that such good works, such *New Creation* behavior, would be so visible that the watching world would see it and glorify God because of it. In those teachings he alerted his followers of their calling to simplicity, and to identity with the poor, to justice and mercy, to being peacemakers, to the possibility of persecution and slander . . . but in the end what those sermons portray is the design of God's *New Creation* for the human community, God's *New Humanity*, into which they were being called. In a very real sense the whole of the New Testament is our guiding line on what our calling and what our disciplines are to be.

At this point, however, I want us to turn to one of the apostolic writings, which is one very practical and awesome overview of the church, and an accompanying punch list of disciplines that will keep it from being compromised or subverted, i.e., that will give it integrity in its role of being light in the darkness, of being the church that overcomes "the gates of hell."

The particular writing to which I am referring is Paul's Letter to the Ephesians (or perhaps to the church in Asia Minor), in which he spells out for them the critical eschatological purpose of the church in the unfolding mystery of God's saving work in human history. You will find all four of the dimensions of our *algorithm* (listed in chapter 4 above) elucidated in that letter: a passion for the person and work of Jesus, their relationships of mutual love, their responsibility to be bearers of the message to those still in the darkness, and the selfless behavior that is to be present in and through them.

But then . . . his conclusion brings us back to "the gates of hell" reality with which we began this part of our inquiry. Paul, after so awesome a description of what is to be the nature of their role as light in the darkness . . . almost abruptly issues a compelling warning to the effect that there really is an adversary, the devil, who will use all of his subtle schemes and subversions to distract God's sons and daughters of light—his church as the community of the light—from its calling. Satan, Paul teaches, is not so likely to engage in some obvious frontal assault on them as he is to simply engage in those subtle erosions of forgetfulness or compromise that will cause them to be more comfortable in, conformed to, and less countercultural within the context of the darkness in which they live day by day. (Yes, Satan does sometimes provoke dramatic frontal assaults on the church in hostile cultures, but even there he seeks to cause the church to compromise and to drift away from its true calling.)

The Mystery Behind the Mystery

Putting On the Armor of Light

And just how are they to prevail against those cosmic powers, and the spiritual forces of the darkness? The answer: He spells out for them their daily dress as children of the light—not what they *do* but what they *wear*, so that they are authentic as the children of God's *New Humanity*. It is by such integrity as displayed by the wearing of that daily dress that they *are* what they have been called to be, that they display the DNA of the divine nature that is within them. Paul employs the simile of the armor of a typical Roman soldier, which would have been altogether familiar to those to whom he was writing, being the historical period in which the Roman Empire was at its high-water mark, and Roman soldiers were omnipresent in the church's context. He tells the Ephesians (and us) to always be putting on "the whole armor of God" (Eph 6:11). Then he details the pieces—seven of them. For our purpose here, be reminded that these pieces of their dress, or armor, are all the intended evidences of the children of the light, and of the community of the light. Be aware, also, that those seven pieces of the armor of the sons and daughters of the light are interdependent, and no one of the seven pieces is complete without the other six pieces. When any one of these seven is omitted, the believer, and the church, become vulnerable at that point.

And remember also that Jesus taught us that by our fruits we should be known. The seven components of the whole armor give us a profound insight as to those fruits, and of how they reflect the divine nature dwelling in us. So let's see if we can get a good working grasp of those seven pieces of our dress as the sons and daughters of the light.

First of all, we put on *the belt of truth*. The primary piece of the soldier's armor is that belt or girdle, because the rest is dependent on it, not to mention its protective role. That one is easy. Jesus is the center of our faith and he has identified himself as the *Truth*, and he also identified his Word, his teachings, as the truth, which truth, when kept, sets men free indeed, i.e., brings everything into focus, and gives the ultimate meaning for which our hearts long.

The sons and daughters of the light are those whose center, and whose object of worship, is Jesus Christ, the Truth. They are those for whom Christ's teachings are the truth, which is the guiding line of their lives.

The *second* piece of the armor is *the breastplate of righteousness*. Basically, that piece of the armor refers to the righteous behavior of the sons and daughters of light, their conformity to the divine nature, and to the teachings of Jesus. *Righteousness* is a huge word in the biblical narrative, but it always somehow reflects "getting it right" and being in conformity with the design of God. Occasionally it is almost a synonym for *salvation* in New Testament writings. This is a key piece of the armor since it defines how we deport ourselves as *New Creation* people in the "stink and stuff" of daily life, i.e., it is the *praxis* of God's *New Humanity*. The apostle Peter wrote to Christ's people under persecution that they are to so live their lives under such assaults that their very behavior will incite the curiosity of those seeing them. "*Now who is there to harm you if you are zealous for what is good?*" (1 Pet 3:13). Righteousness is the *lifestyle* of the sons and daughters of light, even in the most unlikely circumstances and settings. It is what the watching world sees.

Ah yes, but following the breastplate of righteousness is the *third* piece of the armor, which is what the soldier wears on his feet: "*as shoes for your feet . . . the readiness given by the gospel of peace* (Eph 6:15)." That is a fascinating description in the very term it employs for our gospel, i.e., the *gospel of peace*. The follower of Jesus is, first of all, to be always primed and ready as an agent of the *gospel of peace*. Believers do not assault; they are not fractious or neurotic in their engagement with the world. Rather, the sons and daughters of light are reconcilers. They are agents of the one who came to make peace by his cross, who reconciled us to God by his blood, and has given us the ministry of reconciliation. In the prophet Isaiah's portrayal of the "peaceable kingdom," there is described the recreation of all things, there is total harmony. Our good news, our gospel, is one in which the love of God for even his enemies is incarnate in his sons and daughters. This gospel of peace is wonderfully expressed in the classic prayer by St. Francis of Assisi, "*Lord, make me an instrument of your peace, where there is hatred let me so love, where there is injury . . . pardon, where there is doubt . . . faith, where despair . . . hope, where there is . . . darkness, light, where sadness . . . joy.*" His prayer also includes prayers for the ministries of consolation, of understanding, of love, of self-giving, and of pardoning. The light that is to shine from God's sons and daughters is to be the incarnation of such a gospel of peace.

The Roman soldiers carried with them a full-body shield because enemies frequently threw flaming darts at them, and they could protect their whole body behind the tall shields. Paul understood that one of Satan's most devastating weapons is *doubt*, when all the circumstances seem to be going against us, or when our minds cannot understand the realities of daily life. It is to this end that Paul names as the *fourth* piece of the armor *the shield of faith*, which he specifically instructs them to take up in all circumstances. Our shield is our firm appropriation of Christ's faithfulness to us (not ours to him). In the face of Satan's fiery darts, we say with Paul, "*I know whom I have believed, and I am convinced that he is able to guard until that Day what has been entrusted to me*" (2 Tim 1:12). It is this that has sustained so many, many saints through deeply troubled times.

The *fifth* piece of the armor is *the helmet of salvation*. If the breastplate of righteousness portrays the believer as one whose behavior is reflective of the *New Creation* at work in him or her . . . then the helmet of salvation has to do with *thinking Christianly*. God's people are always called upon to know him, to know his will, to know his calling. They are those who see the use of the mind in the service of God as a critical discipline in their lives of discipleship. They are to worship the Lord with all of their minds, among other elements of worship. Peter spoke of the role of knowledge as instrumental in forming in us all things that pertain to life and godliness (2 Pet 1:3–4). Note again that all of these pieces of the armor are interdependent and interactive. The knowledge of God, and God's *New Creation*, and God's will, are essential to the ability of God's *New Humanity* sons and daughters to be agents of the light, and so to prevail over the schemes of the gates of hell to subvert the church from its mission. When the essence of our calling to be the sons and daughters of light is forgotten, or diluted, or displaced . . . then Satan has succeeded in subverting the church from its essence. We are a people with an authority and a guiding line that are found in the teachings of the Word of God, thus the necessity of the helmet of salvation.

The *sixth* piece of the armor is the described as *the sword of the Spirit, which is the Word of God.* This piece of the armor is also often misunderstood, primarily because of two different Greek words that are both translated as "word." One is the Greek word *logos*, which has more of a theological or philosophical meaning, and which has to do with essence or divine principle, and is used by John in speaking of Jesus as the Word, or the *logos*, of God dwelling among us. But the word used here in this passage, in this description of the armor of the believer, is the Greek word *rhema*, which conveys speaking, or uttering, or communicating. In this image, then, an essential piece of the armor is the believer's ability to communicate his or her faith. Peter told the persecuted believers that they should live their lives so that others would become curious and ask about the hope that they were expressing. Peter tells the Christian folk that they were to be ready to give a thoughtful answer with all gentleness and sensitivity (1 Pet 3:15–16). That is what *rhema* is all about: communicating or articulating one's faith in Christ somewhat convincingly. That seems to be the purpose of this image of the sword of the Spirit here—not only a defensive weapon but a weapon for offense. The sons and daughters of light need to be articulate, thoughtful, sensitive, and alert to the reality of those with whom they have contact, in friendly or hostile settings, as actually being those *motherless children*, those inquirers who are looking for something to give them meaning and hope. Such a weapon is our ability to communicate to others what God has done in Christ, and for us individually. That ability, that *sword of the Spirit,* is what the Spirit uses to herald the gospel of God into every corner of the human community in daily contacts and the

The Mystery Behind the Mystery

very real contexts of our lives. The Word of God has many uses in our formation, but here is seems to pertain to the Christian's ability to communicate that Word to whomever.

Then, finally, the *seventh* piece of the armor is that the Christian has the awesome capacity of intimate communication with the God who calls, and that communicating is by the enabling of the Spirit: "*praying at all times in the Spirit, with all prayer and supplication*" (Eph 6:18). The apostle makes this an incredibly wonderful and necessary part of our ability to stand against the schemes of the devil. We have mutual access to God, and we share that with all other believers within the whole global Christian community. When all human help fails, we have such a resource as access to Jesus, our High Priest, and to all of the divine prerogatives of fellowship with the Father, Son, and Holy Spirit. The hymn writer James Montgomery has a wonderful hymn on this warfare, in which he makes the point of the absolute necessity of prayer: "*Undaunted to the field he goes; Yet vain were skill and valor there, Unless, to foil his legion foes, He takes the trustiest weapon: prayer.*"[3]

We initiated this chapter with the reality of the mystery and drama of the church, and it has taken us into the realm of the church as the community of those who are called into God's *New Creation* in Christ . . . but we have immediately realized that this calling is not within neutral territory, but rather that there is that dominion of darkness, or of Satan, that is an existential presence. There is also the promise that those "gates of hell" are not able to withstand the mission of Jesus Christ to build his church, his *New Creation* community. It would be dishonest for us to even try to introduce an answer to the sincere question "*What on earth is the church?*" without spelling out that there is a huge drama taking place in human history, and that Jesus and his *New Humanity* are the communal presence of that drama. But then, there is also that very real dominion of darkness out of which the church is called, and that makes the church to always be standing in missionary confrontation with the works of darkness, and to be the incarnation of God's love for this very present scene in which we

---

3. James Montgomery, "Behold the Christian Warrior Stand" (1825).

live. When such a cosmic reality is not understood, then the mission of the church, and the calling of Christ to be his followers, contains a huge blank spot. However, when it *is* understood, it all gets more thrilling, and that is why the very word *gospel*, in Greek, means *"thrilling announcement."* That also means, however, that God's sons and daughters of light, who have been called into his glorious freedom, are never to be indifferent to those still dwelling in their—perhaps sophisticated, or perhaps hopeless—*darkness*. God's sons and daughters are to be the demonstration of the light of God's love for such.

What human history is all about is the *building of Christ's church*, his *New Humanity*. Human history is only the scaffolding within which this building is taking place. The true building is the church.

Now we need to move on to what Christians are to engage in, in both their times of being gathered together and in that other *Monday morning world* in which they are the incarnation of *New Creation* in their 24/7 lives.

— 9 —

THE WORLDLINESS OF WORSHIP

Communities of God's *New Humanity* (which is how we have been describing the *church*) have two distinct but interdependent expressions. On the one hand, the church expresses itself in those who have been called *out of* whatever the darkness looked like in their lives... and called by Jesus Christ *into* a whole new life, in which life they are being recreated into Christ's very likeness. Those persons find one another and express their mutual faith and love in support of one another in all kinds of forms and venues. Such communal expressions are what I will term the "*church gathered*." But then, when Jesus calls such persons to himself, to new life by the Spirit, and to one another in love... he also calls them to be engaged in his mission to demonstrate that calling and that new life in the real stuff of daily life, what ever that brings, in its tragic, its beautiful, its very practical and inescapable demands, and in its many enigmatic realities. That expression of the church I will then term the "*church scattered*."

Those two expressions are totally inter-dependent and inter-animating. Being engaged as the sons and daughters of light in their daily contexts, whether of sophisticated intellectual darkness, or conversely in so much that is broken and ugly and indifferent, takes its toll in both cases. However, being the *church scattered* in such daily realities is the very purpose of our being called to be the children of light. In one very real sense the church is more the church when it is thus *scattered* than it is when such church communities become consumed by their *gathered* times and forgetful of, or distracted from, their mission to walk as children of light in their 24/7 incarnations. The reality is that the *church-scattered* expression should drive it back to its expression as *gathered* in order to be equipped, encouraged, and refreshed for its engagements in the Monday \-morning world, what with all of its human, social, economic, and political, and often intractable realities. We should also be alerted to the fact that there are a whole lot of wonderful, caring, courteous, and creative persons out there who are still *motherless children*, and whom God loves and seeks to set free within his New Creation . . . not to mention all the confused, broken, and hurting folk.

The point here is that the church is anything but otherworldly. The church is very *this-worldly*. The "sweet by and by" may be the church's hope, but meanwhile we are called to engaged in Christ's mission to demonstrate and herald his *New Creation*. The Lord's Prayer petitions God to make his *New Creation* to be coming on earth—what with all of its brokenness and imperfections—as it is in heaven. That's what Jesus' *messianic* mission was all about, i.e., to be making all things new. His *calling out* of a people to be his own is also a calling to be involved with him in that mission, no matter how dire and humanly impossible it may seem in so many contexts. Full disclosure: There has always been that proclivity in the church's celebrations to seek escape from that scene of darkness, and to focus on some kind of spirituality, or religious expression, and so to be distracted from its missionary calling to walk as children of light here and now, and to be the agents of God's grace and love in the very corners of this present world.

That is to say, that there is so much that flies under the rubric of "worship" that has little to do with the real purpose of worship. Songs and hymns that dwell on heaven (as though our very calling here and now were somehow a scene from which we only wish to escape) are worrisome—even though our great hope is on the

The Worldliness of Worship

consummation of all things at the end of the age, when Christ shall have delivered up his kingdom to God his Father, and God will be "all and in all" (1 Cor 15:28).

Parenthetically, there was an aberration on the Christian message early in the church's history in which some were denying the real humanity of Jesus, and so declared that he was only another non-corporeal religious figure. The church quickly labeled that as a tragic error and an aberration, and reasserted its faith that in Jesus Christ God took on true humanity in order to bring about his *New Creation*. "*And the Word became flesh and dwelt among us*" (John 1:14).

Those called through the Door (which Door is Jesus Christ) are called to be his glory in the realities of the Monday-morning world. They are called to be "his own glory and excellence" (2 Pet 1:3) in the here and now of real ministry, where the darkness is often very real. The church's *gathered* times are primarily to equip us for that calling. Of course the family of God can enjoy all kinds of fun and socialize together . . . but it has the necessity of that which is called *worship*[1] as an essential discipline of keeping itself energized, excited, hopeful, and equipped for its incarnation as *scattered*, wherever that incarnation might be—cutting lawns, doing neurosurgery, parenting precocious children, being a checkout clerk at a store, laboring to survive in marginal economies, creating totally new concepts in Silicon Valley—whatever and wherever.

God knew of this need when he called the children of Israel out of Egypt, and called them to be "a nation of priests" at the foot of Mt. Sinai (Exod 19:6). He gave them his guidelines for their lives and how he intended them to live in fulfilling that calling. The Ten Commandments begin with a focus on God himself—who he is, and as the one who had called them. Then he gave them the weekly discipline of stopping everything else, and reflecting on the one true God who had called them for such a purpose. The brief Ten

---

1. *Worship* is a word whose roots carry the meaning of something like giving honor to worth. It is a word that speaks of dwelling on, or reflecting on, the object of that worth, and responding appropriately.

Commandments defined who they were to be, and to what positive intent he had called them to live in all of their relationships. That command to stop everything one day a week, and to worship, was the *Sabbath rule*. When the Israelites became indifferent to that Sabbath rule, they began to be conformed to all of the other subtle influences of the cultures—and it went downhill from there. The rhythm of life was that of worship and then work.

The church that Jesus is creating (and in its first generations) adopted that same principle, though the church had moved away from some pieces of Judaism. Rather than worshipping on the seventh day, they seem to have adopted the first day of the week (the day of Christ's resurrection) as their time to be together, even though the first day of the week for them was a workday in many cultures. Christians found a way to get together even when they were being persecuted and harassed. They often had to be very clandestine in their gatherings. What they knew was that they needed each other. They needed the encouragement, support, nurture, and relational love of the gathered community. The gatherings may have been (and most commonly were) in homes, and around common meals, but they were very purposeful, and were communities formed in and by prayer. But look what they produced! In a very short time there were followers of Jesus even in Caesar's household, and across the Roman Empire.

What Did the Church Do When Gathered?

In that the New Testament documents were written to churches in several diverse localities, they are all addressed to small colonies of Christ's followers, which seem to have been primarily meeting in homes, where it was virtually impossible for anyone present to be a stranger, or unknown to the rest. There certainly wasn't any focus on the church as an institution. It was all so new. Those small colonies were sort of like our current start-up businesses, in that they were always inventing and then reinventing themselves as they went along in order to most effectively accomplish their mission and purpose. Churches were dynamic colonies of folk who had to be very self-aware of their calling, and to frequently deal with all kinds of interpersonal needs and conflicts and aberrations along the way. There are few clues about any rigid form determining their gathered times, but there are a few that are very revealing, and most helpful for our quest here.

There are some fascinating clues that seem to have been common denominators for them. The first clue is the *one-another* factor, which crops up all through the New Testament. Jesus initially told his disciples that the world would know that they were his disciples as they loved *one another*, and then defined that as the same kind of love as that which the Father had for him. In the apostolic writings, you get a whole spectrum of reminders that the believers were not only to love one another, but to confess their sins to one another, to be subject to one another, to bear one another's burdens . . . and in so many very practical ways to demonstrate a community of reconciled and caring relationships—which you may recall from an earlier chapter is one of the four components of the *algorithm* that demonstrates *New Creation* communities.

That kind of *one-another* intimacy is hardly possible in a large and impersonal assembly in which one can be lost in the crowd. That becomes apparent in the apostle's word to the church at Colossae about some of the realistic components of *one-another* love, like the reality that others can, indeed, be a painful burden . . . yet are to be the objects of ones self-giving love (Col 3:12–14). It is the dynamic of their mutual, caring, burden-carrying love that created expressions of God's *New Humanity*. It is that dynamic that also demonstrates the very image of God being formed in each person's Spirit-empowered life.

A second clue as to what they did when they were together comes from a bit of instruction given to the same church in Colossae: "*Let the word of Christ dwell in you richly, teaching and admonishing one another in all wisdom, singing psalms and hymns and spiritual songs, with thanksgiving in your hearts to God*" (Col 3:16–17). Those in the colonies of God's *New Humanity* were to teach and encourage one another with the Word of Christ, and were to be mutually formed by that same Word. The Word of Christ was to be the rich diet that equipped those persons for their engagement when they were scattered. Yes, and it also gives us a great clue as to the significant place that music and praise has always had when Christians gather for worship. That also gives us a clue as to every believer's role as part of the *one-another* ministry.

The third clue is never spelled out in detail as to exactly how it was accomplished, but when Jesus was with his disciples at the Passover meal, just before his arrest and crucifixion, he instituted the new Passover meal in which the wine represented his blood and the bread his flesh. He told them that when they (he didn't designate how many) were together they should eat the bread and drink the cup in remembrance of him. That was obviously done, and again probably in homes, and perhaps with a communal meal around a table. Paul rehearsed that necessary practice in a complicated issue having to do with the church in Corinth, and gave us what have become the "*words of institution*" for this meal, which has been designated as the "*Eucharist*" (i.e., "giving thanks") or the "*Lord's Supper.*" It appears to have been an essential part of their gathered times, however it might have been observed. The Eucharist is the *gospel* made visible. It is the thrilling message of Jesus Christ, in which Christ becomes present in the bread and the wine.

Those three clues, then, for our inquiry: one-another love; the Word of Christ shared richly in a mutual time of encouragement, instruction, and praise; and the observance of the Eucharist. The purpose of our gathered times of worship is to be encouraged, to be equipped, and to be, in a very real sense, *re-evangelized*. Those mutual disciplines were all to prepare the colony for the week before it. It is never intended to be spiritual entertainment, and it is never escapism. It is to be an encounter with the Lord, who calls men and women to be conformed to his likeness, and to be engaged in his mission. It is important to insert at this point that there was also something like a rite of entrance into the new life in Christ, and that is the church's practice of *water baptism*. It was part of Jesus' initial missionary mandate to his followers (Matt 28:18-20). Again, how and where that was done is never described, but colonies of Christ's followers over the intervening centuries have found, and do find, meaningful ways to administer baptism to those who come into new life through Christ.

A Pattern for the Colonies' Worship Began to Emerge

In the later centuries the church saw in another Scripture passage a pattern for their times of worship, which worship flows from an intimate encounter with God. The prophet Isaiah, from the eighth century BCE, according to his written account, was in the temple at a very stressful time in the nation of Israel's decline, and after the death of its king (cf. Isaiah 6). As Isaiah was there in the temple he had some kind of an overwhelming epiphany, or encounter with God, that was so awesome and terrifying that he fell on his face and realized how totally imperfect and unworthy he was, confessing his personal guilt as well as his involvement in the corporate guilt of the nation. God heard his cry, and, again in a symbolic way, touched Isaiah's lips with a coal from the altar, and declared him cleansed. Next, God gave an invitation to mission, asking, "Whom shall I send, and who will go for us?" (Isaiah 6:8).

Isaiah responded with an act of devotion and dedication by asking God to send him for whatever was that mission. Here it gets interesting (especially as our chapter here is entitled "The Worldliness of Worship"): God told Isaiah that he was sending him to engage in a totally impossible task. He wanted to send his Word to the Israelites, who were able neither to hear what he was saying nor or even to conceive, or see, anything Isaiah would be telling them. They would be totally indifferent. It was to such a spiritually deaf and blind people that God would send Isaiah. How's that for a mission? "Go speak my message plainly to this people, but they have no capacity to hear what you are saying." And yet, Isaiah's message is profoundly *gospel*. It is filled with the message that the sovereign God is the Lord of all, and that he is going to irresistibly and ultimately send his uniquely anointed Servant to accomplish a cosmic, or eschatological, reconciliation of the world to God, and that he would accomplish such by the suffering and dying of his Servant, his anointed. The episode concludes with God giving Isaiah his *instructions*.

With that passage from Isaiah before it, the church over time created an order of worship that walks through the same pattern: 1) a vision of God, or *adoration*; 2) the *confession of sin* and need and inadequacy; 3) the act of divine forgiveness, or *absolution*; 4) the *invitation* to God's mission; 5) the act of response and *dedication* to obedience in the calling; and finally 6) the *instruction* or teaching of Isaiah about the content of the message. Such a calling always begins with adoration, and all else in worship flows out of that encounter. That pattern is used in a large segment of the Christian community in the world[2] . . . but it can also become reduced to mere pageantry and otherworldliness, unless one always keeps in mind that its purpose, as with Isaiah, is to be engaged in the mission of God—one of the four dimensions of our *algorithm*.

It is important to reflect again on the very imperfect context in which we live, and in which the church exists. In Isaiah's day, Israel had all of the accoutrements of religion. They had the temple and its priesthood. They had all of the rites and observances, and the national *hubris*. Their problem was that they had forsaken *Sabbath*, and in so doing had made it all into external religion that had almost no effect on their calling to be a holy nation, or to seek justice, or to be stewards of the land, or to do honor to the name of their God. They became strangers to God, even though they had the impressive temple institution, and they mistakenly assumed that because the temple was there they could live life to their own pleasure, while mistakenly trusting that God would preserve the

---

2. This progression is the basis for the Roman Catholic Mass, and was adopted in some form by the early reformers for many of the Protestant groups. At the same time, it is also an invaluable resource for personal and small-group worship.

nation. They had forgotten and forsaken the covenant by which they were constituted as a nation. They trusted in the symbols but not in the reality that they were to be, in fact, a light to the nations.

We also have, especially in our Western world, many symbols and institutions of religion that exist under the banner of being the church, but which in actuality frequently have nothing to do with what Christ's *New Humanity* is called to be and to do. It takes discernment to distinguish the real from the counterfeit. Many such institutions may have begun with real integrity. It is worth establishing here, however, that Jesus is not creating his church to make us more religious, but rather to make us more truly human, i.e., his *New Humanity*. The church's calling is all about Christ's purpose to be creating us as sons and daughters of light. It is a calling to a very *this-worldly* incarnation, a calling to make real in us truly human in the actual world in which we operate.

All of that is to say that when the church is *gathered* it is to be burnishing its whole armor (which we described in the last chapter), so that when it is *scattered* it can have integrity, and shatter the darkness and stand against the destructive schemes of the devil. It is to be encouraged in such a calling, and be equipped for its mission. The church *gathered* is to be not so much an *inspirational* gathering as a *transformational* gathering, so that, in turn, it can be transformational in it expression as the church *scattered*. Its witness to Jesus Christ is to be instrumental in setting men and women free to incarnate the sheer joy and love and hope that are the aroma of the God's *New Humanity*. With this calling and vision the church then needs to be continually reinventing itself, lest it become forgetful and follow a familiar path into obsolescence.

There is an old and familiar hymn in the church's repertoire that spells out the context and defines our *worldly* calling. On the one hand, the hymn declares, "*This is my Father's world. He shines in all that's fair.*" In that line the church celebrates the good, true, and beautiful in the world into which we are called. But in another verse the hymn states the obvious: "*and though the wrong seems oft so strong, God is the Ruler yet.*"[3] Yes, both. All of the above. The

---

3. Maltbie Babcock, "This Is My Father's World" (1901).

church's worship can be evaluated as to how it equips God's *New Humanity*, not for some *spiritual world* into which to escape, but for their daily lives in the existential realities as God's church *scattered*. That engagement in the daily realities then drives us back to worship with the church *gathered*, to be together, and to know that we are not alone in our pilgrimage. It is that we are to be held accountable for our lives, and to be responsible for those others who are fellow children of light with us. Worship, in that sense, must be very this-worldly, and those who are leaders must never let that urgent need to fade to the margins.

What on earth is the church? It is the community of a whole new race, a *New Humanity*, that is being formed into that which God intends his people to be, and to demonstrate his communal provision among those still without God and without hope in the world. Look, then, for the four dimensions of our *algorithm* and you will be on the right track in the quest to know what on earth the church is to be. The church is a huge gift of God, as God has created, and is creating, a whole new family born of the love of God.

—— Epilogue ——

THE CHURCH: THE AROMA OF CHRIST

What I have written in these pages is the result of a question asked of me innocently, and out of honest curiosity, by my table partner in my favorite coffee shop when he learned that I had been a pastor in the church for decades: "Mr. Henderson, pardon me, but just what is the church?" That question precipitated in me the realization that there are many, especially in the emerging generation, who have had literally no contact with the church. That meant for me that if I were to explain the church to such a person I would have to begin at *square one*. It also meant that I would have to at least attempt to avoid all of the in-house terminology and jargon that has been so much a part of my own experience. I confess that it is all too easy for me to become altogether too abstruse in attempting to answer such a wonderful question.

The church is an essential component of God's love for his rebellious creation. Jesus didn't come to make men and women religious, but to give them meaning and acceptance and hope in understanding the meaning of their humanity—to make them new. God looks upon those "having no hope and without God in the world" (Eph 2:12), and out of his great love comes in Jesus to reconcile such *motherless children* to himself and to give them the hope and meaning for which their hearts long. That is a miraculous transaction, but it begins with Jesus, who is the Door into this new life, this *New Creation*. The church is the community of those who have entered through Christ, and so become the communal demonstration of that *New Creation* within the larger human community. I've tried to walk us through that in this journey. The church is composed of those who have found, in Jesus, a new center for their lives, an authority, a creative source, a guiding line, and a final goal. Then such men and women find each other, and become supportive and encouraging colonies in their journey.

What demonstrates that *New Creation* reality in them is what we sought to depict in chapter 4 as a fourfold *algorithm*: 1) their mutual focus on Jesus and their adoration of him for who he is, what he taught, and what he did in his suffering and death to give them such new life and freedom; 2) their mutual passion to be his agents in God's eschatological search and rescue mission in the world, i.e., to be the missionary arm of God himself; 3) their love for one another with the same love with which Jesus Christ loves them (what with all their imperfections); and 4) their whole way of living and thinking that demonstrates God's intent for his world, and this carried out in lives of joyous obedience to Christ's teachings.

What all of that produces in the church is the *aroma of Christ*. The church, as God's *New Humanity*, is to smell like Jesus, and to think and behave out of its oneness with him. It makes the church to be literally the "dwelling place for God by the Spirit" (Eph 2:22), in which Christ himself continues to be present, bringing light in the darkness. Jesus taught that we discern true and false prophets by their fruits, but then in his teaching he always *segued* right into a description of those fruits that are the evidence of his true disciples, i.e., the *praxis* of his New Creation people.

What is interesting is that Jesus and his apostles, in the New Testament writings, never speak of the *form* of the church. They only speak of the inner dynamics that make it to be the Body of Christ, demonstrated in such colonies or communities of those who have come into this new life through Christ the Door. Try to trap that calling into an institution, or into a denomination, or some external form seeking security, permanence, and familiar sameness . . . and all you succeed in doing is moving the focus from the church's intended purpose, and you have already begun to subvert it from its primary calling, and its participants will soon probably become immunized to the dynamic of *New Creation* and usually begin the slide into ecclesiastical ossification. The authentic church is great at doing "end runs" in unexpected ways and places, and in so doing proving that the gospel is always thrillingly out of control. It is Christ who is building his church, and when what is ostensibly a church loses its focus there will inevitably emerge an unexpected new colony of those faithful to their calling.

Put together three or four of Christ's followers, or some small number of those who have come into this new life, and they will come up with some communal form of mutual support, of practical love, of encouragement, of edification, of mutual teaching and admonishing, plus accountability to each other. Inhabited by the Holy Spirit, such innovative colonies will incarnate Christ's passion and love for this present scene and its inhabitants, who are captive to the darkness . . . those still without hope and without God in the world. Such colonies, when healthy, will be contagious, growing, ever dividing and multiplying, like leaven, as they irresistibly draw others to the light and make disciples. Those colonies will reinvent themselves in different and changing social and cultural settings. They will not seek permanence, only obedience to their calling by Christ.

The Church Is a Rich Tapestry, or a Magnificent Mosaic

What on earth is the church? The church is like a rich tapestry, or a mosaic, with a seemingly endless interaction of figures and colors. It takes on innumerable forms as it becomes light and leaven in innumerable settings, and in ever-changing contexts. The church emerges in unexpected places and in unexpected forms, but there is no set form. The church is elastic and versatile. There are some inner patterns that we have discussed above. It faces inevitable challenges. Yet the form never determines the church's authenticity. Its authenticity is known by its fruits, and in our journey in this book, it is known by its faithfulness in the fruits defined by our fourfold *algorithm*.

Those who come into proximity should sense life, the aroma of what their hearts and minds long for—not some kind of safe or stagnant religion, but rather to the key to the mystery of life. They should see the evidences of the divine nature being created, the fruits of the new life in the Spirit—not perfect but unmistakable . . . or as the psalmist portrayed them, they are those who, in the realities of each day, "As they go through the Valley of Baca they make it a place of springs" (Ps 84:6).

What on earth is the church? It is two or three, or many, who through Christ (the Door) have been set free to be a part of God's truly human people, his new race of humankind who are being formed into his image.

But a disclaimer is necessary here, also. All that being said about the church, it is certainly not immune to all the crappy and haphazard stuff, or to destructive persons that always seem to infiltrate it. The church continues to exist in a broken world. Yes, there have also been casualties along the way, and contradictions, as well as counterfeits and charlatans. The New Testament is very realistic about all of this . . . which is exactly why we must return again and again to the vision of the community of God's *New Creation* in Christ, and those four dimensions of our *algorithm* as an aid. We must always be searching Scripture because it is our authority and our guiding line. Then we must look for those who model such.

Look and you will find such colonies in such a diversity of places. Yes, sometimes you find them inhabiting venerable old church institutions, but you may also find them around the table at your local coffee shop, or in concentration camps in countries where the Christian faith is outlawed. You will find them most often in homes. Sometimes they collaborate with other colonies and meet periodically in rented or leased rooms. But their guarantee is that they are the creation of the Holy Spirit, and that they are continually being birthed in order to bring light and hope to this world which God loves. All who profess to have embraced Christ, by their very baptism, are a dynamic part of that mission—even (maybe especially) those in modest and difficult settings.

The church is how and where Jesus is incarnated in the here and now of this age. Such churches are communities of the *Age to Come*. It is in the equipping of each participant, and the encouragement of them in this pilgrimage, that the church is a necessary component in true discipleship.

What on earth is the church? Listen carefully: Near the end of his earthly ministry, Jesus said to his infant church, which was composed of his followers, "*As the Father has sent me, even so I am sending you*" (John 20:21). The awesome ministry of inaugurating God's *New Creation*, which was his mandate from the Father, he would soon be making possible by his death and resurrection, and he assigned to his followers the very same mandate that the Father had given to him. They would be those who incarnate God's *New Humanity*. The church was to be a sweet aroma of Christ to the world.

That's what on earth the church is all about.

www.ingramcontent.com/pod-product-compliance
Lightning Source LLC
Chambersburg PA
CBHW070926160426
43193CB00011B/1590